THE PR Bidie
Marketing

*Proven Secrets of the Pros
for Winning Marketing Strategies
that Get You Work!*

STEVE STEPHENS

BONUS CHAPTER BY ALLISON HESTER

GUARANTEED · PROVEN · RESULTS

www.stevestephens.biz

ISBN 1453859101
Printed in the United States of America

www.stevestephens.biz

INTRODUCTION

Congratulations on your decision to take charge of your financial health!

You are holding in your hands a true blueprint for a secure future. I am sure you have heard that the longest journeys are conquered one step at a time. You have taken that first step.

The information within these pages will transfer the knowledge you need to grow and maintain a thriving pressure cleaning business to prosperity. Knowledge is not power. Knowledge is *potential* power. Knowledge that remains idle is worthless. This book, without action, is worthless.

When knowledge takes action and meets or makes opportunity, success is inevitable. Bottom line, *you* make it happen!

I cannot make you get up in the morning and choose to succeed. I can't make you look at an obstacle and find a solution, or better yet, an opportunity. I can't make you get this book out of your junk drawer and get busy. What I can do is guarantee your success once you decide to succeed. I can be your success coach and give you the formula for proven results.

If you are not getting all the sales you desire, then take the second step. Make an executive decision right now to follow this recipe, and you too will find the magic.

STEVE STEPHENS

Steve Stephens is the owner and founder of HydroTech Pressure Cleaning Technologies, Inc., the HydroTech Training Facility for pressure cleaning contractors, and Steve Stephens Consulting. Through his school, consulting services, and publications, Steve has assisted hundreds of businesses get a jumpstart on success. He has also had the privilege of contributing to the success of HydroTech-certified companies throughout North America.

Steve is nationally recognized as one of the top experts in the industry and has countless published works to his credit. He is also a contributing writer and consultant for *Cleaner Times* magazine and contributing author to the *Power Washer's Guidebook, Marketing Your Power Washer Services* and other industry publications. His company, HydroTech, Inc., was featured on the cover of *Pressure Concepts* magazine as a model of integrity, character and image.

Steve has been in the pressure washing industry since 1980, and previously served on the Board of Directors for the Power Washers of North America (PWNA) and as chairman of the Technical Support Network. He also served as a featured speaker at several PWNA meetings and as PWNA keynote speaker in 2001 and 2010.

Steve contributes his success to an ongoing commitment to excellence, research and development, and the desire to help others succeed. He takes a personal interest in the growth and reputation of the pressure cleaning industry.

ALLISON HESTER

Allison Hester was introduced to the pressure cleaning industry in 1994 when she joined the staff of *Cleaner Times* magazine. She served as the managing editor from 1994 to 1998, then rejoined the staff in 2009. In addition to overseeing the magazine's editorial content, she was instrumental in the development of industry publications such as *The Power Washer's Guidebook.* She also authored the popular "History of the Pressure Washing Industry" series.

Prior to *Cleaner Times*, Allison worked in advertising and promotions, first for the local NBC affiliate and later as creative director for a local advertising agency. In 1998, she left *Cleaner Times* to work as communications manager for a large, not-for-profit healthcare organization. In this role, she developed and managed numerous award-winning marketing and communications projects. She also became a certified corporate trainer in intercultural communications.

In 2000, Allison left her corporate job to become a freelance writer and graphic designer. Since then, she has worked with clients from around the country in a variety of industries and communications roles. She has also worked on projects with several pressure cleaning professionals to help them enhance and grow their businesses.

Allison is currently completing her Master's in Interpersonal and Organizational Communications at the University of Arkansas Little Rock.

TABLE OF CONTENTS

"The Fastest Path to Success is by Helping Others to the Next Level."

– Steve Stephens

Chapter *1*

The Setback

Top: This was taken about 1/4 mile from our office. Notice that the farther you go, the deeper the water gets.

Bottom: Pulling the raft behind me about 1/2 mile from our facility.

Our Raleigh, NC-based office was a quarter-mile away in the middle of a newly formed "lake" created by Hurricane Fran. As I looked upon the aftermath, my emotions were irrational and I was determined to get to my "life's work."

My friends and family begged me to give it a few days and let the water calm and lower. But from my irrational viewpoint it looked safe – just a long way to paddle. I could really see no danger, just a long walk in three- to-four-feet deep water. Then I knew, of course, it would get deeper and become more challenging when it came time to cross the creek that now was a strong, fast current river. However, it only appeared to be a short cross. I could do it. I *had* to do it.

After wading through the chilling water, the earth disappeared from under my feet. I jumped into the toy raft I had bought for 29 dollars. I used a piece of wood I had found floating for a paddle. The current became stronger and I had to hold onto trees emerging from the water to keep my path. I wasn't expecting this.

I pushed my raft forcefully away from the tree and used my piece of wood as a makeshift rudder. The current now was scary and moving me at a running pace. I grabbed a piece of heavy rubber that emerged from the water to hold my course and catch my breath. It was a huge CB antenna from a truck that was under water. I held on with all my might and decided to turn back. I looked back at the way I had come and there was a picnic table, a cooler and several plastic 50-gallon trashcans racing past by the strong force of the water. I was at least a football field length away from safety. There would not be a return, not from the way I came.

My hands were getting sore from the thin antenna and I was looking desperately for my next move. About 50 feet away was a big tree with all sorts of vines hanging down. If I could get a break in the current, I could make those vines and rest while the tree anchored my raft. The current seemed to slow down so I paddled with everything in me toward the tree with the vines. The slowness of the current must have been an illusion since I didn't see the debris passing me by.

I passed the tree with the vines with no hope of grabbing anything. The current now had me and I was at the mercy of the water.

I saw another tree about 70 feet ahead and about 20 feet to the right as I was racing with the flow of the current. I slipped the rope that was tied to the raft around my shoulder. Racing with the current, I paddled with all my might toward the tree. I could tell I was going to miss the tree by a good 15 feet, so I dropped my wood and dove out of the raft to the tree. The combination of my jump, kicks and current got me close enough to catch hold of a kudzu vine and pull myself toward the tree. Water was raging past me now holding my body firmly centered on the tree. The nylon rope from the raft was around my shoulder and I was caught with it cutting under my chin. The force was unbelievable, but I felt a thick branch under the water and locked my legs around it with desperation. I was secure.

I pulled my raft back up to me and tied in to the branch beneath. My muscles were burning and all I could think of was relief. I was OK. My heart was pounding through my chest, but all I could think was "I'm OK. Give me a minute. Just let me rest. I'm safe. I'll be OK. Just give me a minute."

THE REALITY

As I gained my composure and my wits, I took note of my surroundings. I was now at the edge of what used to be a creek, now a raging river with white waters collecting and devouring everything in its course.

Holding onto the branch, all that remained above water were my head and my shoulders. Lumber, gas cans and tree limbs violently swept by my face. Just a moment without attention to the oncoming debris would knock me out for sure.

Suddenly I'm wondering. "Why in the world am I here? What can I possibly do to help anything?"

I looked across what once was a trickling creek at the white water taking everything in its path. I looked closely and across the river about 150 feet I could see the antenna of one of our company trucks. I looked on and I could see a ladder that was on a rack atop one of our hot-water trailer units. My heart sank.

I then focused on the back rear door of our building. Water was above the doorknob. My mind felt so scrambled. It looked as though someone had taken our building, our business and everything we owned and put it in the middle of a lake.

Water raced against my face. The force, along with the view, seemed overwhelming. I felt like my life was over. I thought I wanted to die.

The water was pulling me so hard all I could feel was numbness, emptiness and defeat. I wanted to just let go and let the cold forceful waters devour me as it had everything else I owned. Everything that I had worked for, for so many years had been ravaged and destroyed by this monster. Oh my God, what was I going to do?

Now getting to the office did not seem so important. The reality of my position got my attention. I had been fooled by the large tree lines that kept the white waters a secret from the distance. Well, it was no secret now!

I would have never believed what I was getting myself

into. Only a fool would knowingly attempt such a ridiculous task. I am no fool. Persistent maybe, but still I felt foolish. What would be said by the many who begged me not to attempt this ridiculous mission? What an embarrassing way to die! I even thought about what they would say on the news.

I had before me the challenge to survive. I could see clearly, the only way across was to calm down, think and make each move count.

I tried again to clear my mind and strategize my way across as if I was playing pool – setting up my moves a couple of steps in advance. My first move was to get in the raft. That was better because then my perception was from a higher level without dodging the debris being fired in my face.

I plotted my course. From up the river came a big piece of 2 by 4. It looked about 16 feet long. I reached up, broke off a branch and quickly hit the 2 by 4 coming toward me. I got it! Now I had a raft, rope and 2 by 4 to conquer this river. The odds were getting better.

I plotted my route to safety in three moves. The first was another tree about 30 feet across and about 85 feet down the river. I reached under the water to untie my raft as I pushed away with all my strength across the current. I then took my

My Resting Place. This picture was taken a week after the flood. You can still see the mud on top of the hood.

16

2 by 4 and pushed off another tree and, before I knew what was happening, I had caught hold of my target with dear life. I thanked God for kudzu that gave me the lifeline I needed to get to that tree. I was then over halfway to safety.

I lost my 2 by 4 but regained my hope. Now in the midst of the charging water, I felt like a turtle in the middle of the highway. Logs, tires, shelves, anything that wasn't tied down from the business up river was coming crashing at me. This wasn't a place to ponder. This was a place to die.

Without regard to my next move, I dove again out of the raft to a huge fallen tree that had been uprooted by the hurricane. My reach was short and under the water I went. Speeding in the blackness of the murky water, I was merely another piece of debris, in complete submission to the water that controlled my every move. The rope from the raft pulled me like a can dangling behind a car. I was being slammed against downed and uprooted trees everywhere. I caught a glimpse of one that led to the shore on the other side. I kicked and tried to force my body in that direction. I took hold of a small limb that seemed to be as strong as the tree. I knew it was going to break, but it only bent.

I pulled myself closer to the tree with the branch holding all of my weight, the force of the water and the heavy drag of the raft. I was pulling, struggling and using every bit of energy I could muster to get myself closer to the large branch from which the small one had grown. Every second, my focus was on the limb – waiting for it to snap, planning my next move for when it broke. I continued to pull my way closer to the larger branch. My eyes stayed focused on the small limb where I knew it would break. Closer, closer, closer

I made it to the large branch. I thanked God for the strength he had placed in that small limb that got me there. I then bear hugged the large branch and pulled my way up the tree. Once I got to the tree, I knew I was OK. I pulled the raft in by the rope and followed that tree to the edge of the river until I got beyond the force of the current.

I then started feeling for earth beneath my feet because I knew I was getting close to our rear parking lot. I put the raft in front of me and pushed forward toward our property. A few good kicks and I felt the ground under my feet. I waded over to one of the trucks and felt around for the cab. I climbed up on the top of the cab and rested. I made it. Now what?

LOST HOPE?

I sat on top of the truck empty hearted at all the ruins. I just remained there for a while with disbelief. How could this have happened ? A helicopter flew overhead and life stopped for a while. I stayed idle awhile and broke down inside.

It took me some time to gather up the courage to continue. I rummaged through the debris and mirk and felt for the doorknob to our building under the water. I unlocked and pushed the door open. The first sight I had of our facility was our refrigerator floating in the hallway. One and five gallon containers were floating everywhere. I waded past the bathrooms, where all that was visible were the tops of the sinks and the mirrors. I remember seeing a poster in the men's room that I had put up to motivate everyone. It was a picture of a mountain climber standing at the top of a mountain surrounded by water. It read, "Push yourself to the limits because if you never fail, you will never succeed." (Or something like that.)

Again I wanted to cry, scream, yell or something – but what would help? I turned the corner from the hallway into our workshop. Everything that wasn't floating, hung on the wall or on top of shelves was destroyed. Again, I saw a picture I had bought from Successories: "Success is a

journey, not a destination." This had a picture of a canoe in the water. This was one journey I was not ready for.

I tried to take inventory the best I could, but it was just impossible. The silence was ringing in my ears. The only sound was of the wading and moving of water as I pressed forward. No one else in their right mind had even come

to their place of business because the media said it was impossible. They were right. I had really been dumb to go to the office.

I looked around. It seemed that most everything I found belonged to other people. Most every unit in our workshop belonged to other contractors who had trusted us to repair them. What was I going to do? Not everyone got hit by Hurricane Fran like we did. To a few, it was business as usual and I knew they were going to want their machines.

I don't know why, but I had to walk into the two new offices we had just added on and completed the day before. New carpet had just been put in. We had just finished putting up our pictures, hooking up our computers and personalizing the offices with items that were now all beneath the putrid muddy water.

It finally hit me – *the smell*; I was choking to breathe and my mouth watered. I walked through to our receptionist's office and into the showroom. The equipment that was bright and shiny and the envy of many was now submerged in the deep disgusting water that reeked of sewage. No one envied it now. The showroom was the room that was most shallow with water, so I sat on the table and looked out the window.

I wasn't the only victim of this disaster; just the only one with a screw loose enough to venture out. There was the printing shop next door, a hair salon, a sign shop, a Goodyear store and a Subway across the street. Behind us was a Cadillac dealer and a Chinese restaurant. All were total losses. Down the street was a Kmart. They bulldozed it down. A Mazda dealership, Nissan dealership and a used car lot. All cars gone. Flooded. Completely submerged.

I spent about 25 minutes taking all this in and decided I could take no more. It was time to go. On the way out, I was adding the dollars in my head as I saw computers, office equipment, cleaning equipment, chemicals and so many pressure-washing units that were destroyed. It was overwhelming.

Getting back to safety would be easy now because I knew to avoid the creek. I waded out in the chilling water in front

> "The difference between an amateur and a professional is that an amateur gives up when encountering difficulties and a professional speeds up."

of the building into the street. Water was up to the bottom of the "No Parking" signs. I held onto my raft and let it carry me about a quarter of a mile down the street until it was shallow enough to walk. I pulled my raft behind me.

Now what? How was I supposed to deal with this? We had no flood insurance. We were only renting our property, and only the owners of that area knew there was a possibility of that kind of flood. What now? Back home? No electricity, no phone. It would be three days before the water would be low enough for officials to actually let us into the area. For real, life was put on hold.

A DIFFERENT POINT OF VIEW

Life would always be different after that day. I will always remember the freedom that being debt-free gives. No worrying about a mortgage, vehicle payments, equipment payments, no money worries at all. I had worked smart all my life, putting away a little money all the time. I had always managed my money by Biblical principles. The fact about money and its Biblical principles is that it doesn't matter if you believe them or not, they work.

I can hold a 700 pound rock over your foot. You don't have to believe it will hurt if I let go. But, it will.

It didn't take long to go through a few hundred thousand dollars trying to get back on my feet. True colors are revealed vy individuals when you are knocked down and have lost your money and your ability to help them. Companies you have done business with for years suddenly have policy changes. Some you thought to be your friends were actually only there while the profits were high and the risk was low.

The days of calling the bank and having them deposit 50 grand in my account until I got back in town were over. I actually borrowed money on my house once the savings had been depleted. Not before I ran up several thousands of dollars on credit cards.

I will never forget the days of cleanup that followed. Writing check after check to contractors that had left their units with us for repair. No flood insurance bred our path to the future. I will never forget the faces of the multitudes of "power wash" companies that rushed to the opportunity of our misfortune. I thought they had come to help, but one by one they would come to see what we were giving away and what kind of flood sale we would give. These were companies that we extended credit to when others would not. Companies that we loaned equipment to when they could not afford to rent. Companies we had let borrow personal vehicles and company trucks in order for them to do work. These were the companies that broke my heart.

It was my darkest hour...so I thought. I rummaged for days through the mud and filth, never getting used to the vile smell of the sewage. Dumpster after dumpster was filled and removed. It seemed I was all alone. All others were busy getting their lives and their loved ones' lives back together. I thought this was the loneliest time of my life; I will never forget how lonely that time was as I tossed bundle after bundle of my past and future into the dumpsters.

Pictures of jobs that I had done in the eighties all destroyed. Letters from happy customers that were my pride and joy all glued together by the mud and gone forever. Computer files of accounts gone. Hundreds of books I cherished, articles I had written, speeches I had done and so many expensive, large sets of seminar books on tape and CDs. Cases of books that we sold on pressure cleaning repair. Copies of the first edition of the *Power Washer's Guidebook*. (This was a symbol of a new transition in my life as a teacher. Thank you Charlene). So many things could never be the same.

THE MAGIC OF OTHERS

There were many companies in our industry that helped us so much during those first couple of years. I truly don't know what we would have done without their financial and emotional support. Charlene and *Cleaner Times* were and always have been there. They carried us for I know well over a year. We owed them so much money (at least to us) and they stood by us and were always encouraging. The relationship with *Cleaner Times* was and is one I will always hold sacred. They are all GOOD PEOPLE. The hurricane couldn't take that away.

Kop-Coat, the parent company of Wolmans Woodcare basically sent us over $5,000 of inventory and said "pay when you can." I am sure they had no earthly idea it would take almost two years, but they were great. Simpson carried us like a baby. They never missed a shipment to us even though we missed lots of payments to them.

A local company, General Rental, carried us through the shallow waters. They have definitely been like a rock! They are as faithful to our relationship now as they were when we had a generous cash flow. I often wonder if we would have even made it without them. The flood cannot take that away. Thank you Don.

One of my favorite consultants, David Frink, has always been a plane ride away, whether I needed moral support or one of the best instructors in the world for our school on mechanics, engineering and service. If it is broken, he can fix it. If you can dream it, he can design and build it!

We could have never gotten back on our feet without the help of so many other companies and people. When you feel like you have already made it, when you feel like you have the world by the tail, when you feel like you have reached somewhat of a financial success, then the rug is snatched out from under you. That is when humility stares you dead in the eyes. Humble is borrowing money from your in-laws. Humble is borrowing money from your kid brother, your kid sister and your parents, over and over and over again. I am extremely grateful.

TREADING WATER

People are generally surprised to find that the direct impact of Hurricane Fran hit so many years after the flood. The fact is that on impact, we were financially strong. Impeccable credit, hefty savings account, extremely nice home paid for: the future was looking good.

Over the years we have found that Hurricane Fran has resulted in several million dollars in uninsured losses. Why couldn't we get help? What about FEMA? Ask my accountant who had a heart attack and died while working with the IRS on our behalf reconstructing books. Records were destroyed. New accountants. Missed deadlines.

Sometimes, I believe you just have to accept circumstances and keep going. The ironic constant during the whole ordeal is that every legal advisor recommended bankruptcy. It was time to get another advisor.

What is the deal with the world? People talk about bankruptcy like they're making a late payment. Where have our morals gone? If you have filed bankruptcy, I don't know what your baggage was like. I don't criticize you. My heart goes out to anyone who has carried the burden of rude and sarcastic bill collectors. But, I have had so many companies file bankruptcy on us and we get nothing! That's not fair. I have had businesses file bankruptcy, stiff us for three grand and call us the next week to do more work! Have they bumped their cotton-picking heads?

"That's business." Folks, that's not business. That is breaking a promise, plain and simple. If I borrowed 20 dollars from you and promised to pay it back, that is my word. I promised. People can call it "chapter whatever" to sugar coat the truth. Someone broke a promise. Even today, as I am chiseling away at my debt, I get quite a few calls from companies that guarantee that they can make the debt "go away." It does not go away. The entire economy is hurt by such an action, especially the small businesses that trusted us to make good on our handshake.

So I kept pressing forward, and I returned to the basics, and I paid my debt and succeeded. I want to help you do the same.

So let's get started.

HYDROTECH is *the* Industry's Information Source.

HydroTech has been featured on the cover of three issues of *Cleaner Times* magazine for our successful, safe brick cleaning process, and once for our low-pressure, bleach-free wood restoration process.

We have also contributed several articles to *Cleaner Times* and other industry publications.

In December 2009, HydroTech owner Steve Stephens joined the *Cleaner Times* team as a consultant and featured writer.

Steve is also scheduled to serve as keynote speaker for the 2010 Power Washer's of North America (PWNA) annual conference.

All of ths knowledge and experience is available when you put us on your team!

This is an example of how we communicate credibilty to our clients.
Money cannot buy this type of marketing power!

▌ arketing ▌ agic

It is now the information age where messages are sent and received in a matter of seconds. Your customer base or prospect list may all be reached simultaneously by the masses. Contracts and checks can be faxed or submitted online, products are shipped overnight, and services are ordered, scheduled and confirmed via e-mail.

Today, the first impression many companies send is delivered through an automated greeting, sending customers through a robotic series of questions and touch-tone responses. We may be alarmed at the sound of a live voice. We may even be conditioned to prefer leaving a voice mail for fear of having to interact with another human being.

The information age has created extraordinary opportunity. Never have there been so many ways to market your services or products. We are overwhelmed with a multitude of potential marketing money pit choices..

This book is a result of my intense research of marketing through classes, courses, seminars, role models, and books on marketing that date back to the late 1700s and as recent as next-day air. Through these sources and my own experiences, I believe the marketing magic is revealed.

I must also contribute a wealth of this information to

Hurricane Fran, which forced me again to the front line of our business operations. Real people, real emotions, real problems and real situations, and more importantly, real relationships. The types of relationships that require effort from everyday people just like you and me, every day. The revelation of this research and experience is MAGIC. Unfortunately, I would have never discovered the secret from behind my desk.

I've heard that success is often not sighted and embraced because it is often disguised in work clothes. (How true.) Within the magic, we will identify some proven formulas for marketing and sales that are targeted to the pressure cleaning industry. But first, let's look through the smoke and mirrors at the real magic that has worked for centuries.

COMMUNICATING CREDIBILITY

Credibility, or reputation, is possibly the most important contributor to the success and longevity of any business. Some businesses shout from the hilltops about their "honesty" and "good name," yet their actions are so loudly disagreeing that most cannot hear a word they are saying.

How do we achieve credibility? What can we do to make sure our actions match the messages we are sending? We can create systems. That's right, systems. Systems provide businesses with a consistency that guarantees a certain standard. Systems assure us of an accurate expected outcome each time we perform a task. That is why a Big Mac made in Washington tastes so much like the one in Florida.

Systems are a piece of cake. Making your systems work by developing checklists for each operation is not difficult. Whether you're washing a truck, cleaning sidewalks, or recovering and separating water and oil, your system will work if you have a checklist.

Pilots are much more likely not to crash while attempting to land if they use their checklist. Your business is less likely to crash if you not only have a checklist, but also use it.

THE WRITTEN CHECKLIST

Every task or service your business undergoes should have a written, clear and concise checklist. No matter how trivial a service might seem, a checklist – when properly used – will eliminate a wealth of problems and miscommunications.

I know this because I experienced the opposite when I realized our company's systems were not being used by my technicians. Memory was being substituted for a real hand-held checklist, resulting in inconsistencies and an apparent trend of substandard projects. Customers were confused as to what to expect. and being shortchanged for their dollars. Others were getting twice their money's worth while we suffered the loss. All lost in the long run – clients, technicians, office staff and the bottom line. The biggest loss was the unfortunate confusion we placed on our customers of whether they could truly depend on us.

Before we continue, I've included a few checklists that have worked for us. These work in a variety of ways. Once a job is completed, the technician fills out the checklist as s/he inspects the job. By signing the checklist, technicians are giving their word that the project meets our standards.

In our quality control program, we review 25 percent of all work performed. If an inspector finds substandard work, the first thing we do is compare the work order with the checklist.

These checklists are literally foolproof. These can be modified, or you can make new ones that target your specific needs. Just make sure you *use* them! Your company policy should be to read and see every item on the checklist, not just before departure in the morning, but also after every job.

Getting back out on the front line helped me get the systems back in place. Keeping them there required diligence and a sharp quality control system to enforce that the checklists continued to be used.

Thousands can be saved every year just by having the needed tools and parts. For years, I was spending a fortune paying technicians to run and to get items they forgot. There are not many things that make me as mad as when someone has to make a 50-mile round trip because someone forgot the acid injector. " If you don't read your checklist, you're not doing your job! No matter

"Why didn't you read your @#!$%& checklist?!?!?!?"

how trivial a service might seem, a checklist, when properly used, will eliminate a wealth of problems and miscommunications.

A Few Examples of Checklists

This particular checklist is for a service we offer home builders and large general contractors:

Foundation Package Checklist

Check Each Upon Inspection

_____ 1. Examine house from left to right. How is the street appeal?

_____ 2. Check for *any* brick dust on porches, windows, etc.

_____ 3. Is landscaping straw put back perfectly in place?

_____ 4. Are the bushes clean from all dirt and mud?

_____ 5. Did you help the painters out by rinsing all siding?

_____ 6. Are HVAC units, electric, gas meters all free from mud?

_____ 7. Is the deck mud free?

_____ 8. Are patios, stoops, etc., sprayed off and landscaping back in place?

_____ 9. Are all bricks cleaned to HydroTech standards?

_____10. Did you clean the garage walls with low pressure to remove dirt and dust?

_____11. Is the garage door closed and all construction dirt rinsed off?

_____12. Did you perform a HydroTech extra to show appreciation for our customer's business?

_____13. Perform a final walk around.

_____14. Final check – street appeal.

_____15. Always thank the customer. On occasion, get feedback so we can better serve them.

Date: _____

Here is another example of an effective checklist. Notice how nothing is left to chance. Once a technician is trained, if these items are checked off, the project should usually meet a minimum standard.

Dress Up Checklist

Check Each Upon Inspection

_____ 1. Is the front of the house immaculate from the builders' eyes?

_____ 2. Is landscaping straw around the house, walks and drive put back in place?

_____ 3. Are stoops, sidewalks and patios flawlessly clean?

_____ 4. Are all entrances free of dirt, dust, mud, etc.?

_____ 5. Is the deck in showcase condition? NO MUD!

_____ 6. Are all windows and sills squeaky clean?

_____ 7. Is the HVAC and electricity meter unit dirt and dust free?

_____ 8. Are the siding, soffits, and foundation clean?

_____ 9. Do a final walk around. Check for mistakes and left behind tools.

_____ 10. Once again, look at the home through they eyes of the homeowner and the builder. Does this project have your signature on it? If it does, then you have completed the project. The homeowner, the builder and HydroTech will shine!

_____ 11. Remember everything you do, do it to the absolute best of your ability. You are the only sources of success on this job! We have entrusted our future to you. Thank you for being the best you can be!

Date: _____

Here is a before and after picture of a Dress Up Package. Which one of these houses would you like to have your name associated with? Which one do you think will help the builder impress his potential home buyers? ALWAYS make sure your signature is on every project you perform.

The presentation of this home is dramatically improved by a "Dress Up and Drive" Package

This checklist, modified to your business, should eliminate the excuse: "I forgot." It is also very helpful to ensure you always have what you need, even when your mind is in one-thousand other places.

Truck Checklist

Equipment
____ 1ea.: Brush & Pole
____ 1ea.: 7' Wand
____ 1 ea.: Spare Acid Injector
____ 1 ea.: Scraper
____ 1 ea.: Pair of Goggles
____ 1 ea.: Roll of Plastic
____ 2 ea.: 8' Long Steel Extension
____ 1 ea.: Extra Gun
____ 1 ea.: Roll of Duct Tape
____ 1 ea.: Y for Hose
____ 1 ea.: Roll of Teflon Tape
____ 1 ea.: Dental Pick
____ 10 ea.: O Rings (1/4")
____ 20 ea.: O Rings (3/8")
____ 1 ea.: Male Hose Repair
____ 2 ea.: Female Plugs (Large)
____ 3 ea.: Female Plugs (Small)
____ 1 ea: Variable Speed Nozzle
____ 2 ea.: Female Couplers (1/4")
____ 2 ea.: Female Couplers (3/8")
____ 3 ea.: Male Couplers (1/4")
____ 1 ea. Unloader
____ 1 ea.: Unloader
____ 5 ea.: Gallons of Gas

____ 4 ea.: Rubber Water Hose Gaskets
____ 5 ea.: Gallons of Kerosene
____ 1 ea.: Small 3' Wand or Extension
____ 1 ea.: Female Hose Repair
____ 1 ea.: 0, 15, 25, 40 degree Spare Nozzles (6 gpm)
____ 1 ea.: Extension Pole & Brush
____ 1 ea.: High Pressure Hose Repair Connect
____ 1 ea.: 100' Spare High Pressure Hose

Tools:
____ 1 ea.: Small Adjustable Wrench
____ 1 ea.: Large Adjustable Wrench
____ 1 ea.: Pair of Large Channel Locks
____ 1 ea.: Pair of Pliers
____ 1 ea.: Rethreader
____ 1 ea.: Pair of Vice Grips
____ 1 ea.: Set of Screwdrivers
____ 1 ea.: Water Key

Date: _____

Technician Signature: _____

Chapter 3

Details Are Like a Savings Account

Gaining credibility is the utmost of importance in the marketing magic strategy. It is the glue that will hold your company together when you stumble across the mines that might normally blow you off the map, or in our case, out of the water.

Your credibility is an air of everything you and your business are associated with: the building you are in, the people you employ, the technology you use and the attention you pay to your customers. The cleanliness, grooming and manners of your employees also contribute to your credibility, as does the cleanliness and organization of your vehicles and units. The manner in which your company vehicles are driven is also important. A courteous driver may be all it takes to engrave your company's name in a customer's mind. The way your phones are answered can earn you credibility or destroy it like an atomic bomb. These are tiny but high-powered details.

Entire marketing strategies have collapsed because of the lack of attention to seemingly unimportant details. This undermines the prospective client's confidence. Cheap stationery, business cards, door hangers, brochures, typos, misspelled words, and poor English can destroy credibility.

Paper stock can look and feel exquisite and credible, or cheap and fleeting.

Take a look at your direct mailers. Is your signature authentic? Are you telling your customer you don't have time to personally sign a letter to them? If that's the case, you wouldn't possibly have time for them if a problem arose with their service, would you? That may be just what you are communicating if you use a sloppy signature stamp.

Does your entire business remain true to its colors and theme? If you were to lay out your business card, stationery, envelopes, invoices, fax sheets, pictures of your company vehicles, and any trade show or billboard signs you employ all on one table, would they all carry the same logo, colors, theme and slogan? If not, you are probably missing out on the complete impact of your advertising dollars.

These details may seem unimportant. The fact is that over a period of time, these details all work together. Little, consistent details make a profound impact. They may seem subtle at first, yet investing in a long-term, systematic checklist of procedures and designs can provide you with momentum that money cannot buy, and also with enough business not to worry about what money can buy.

> ## "One of Life's Greatest Pleasures is Accomplishing What Others Say You Cannot."

Marketing Credibility

L ook for opportunities to promote your expertise and goodwill in your community. Send helpful newsletters or e-newsletters to your client and prospect base. This will keep your name fresh in their minds. Make sure the newsletters are helpful to them and interesting. Give them something to look forward to. Again, make sure the contents are worth reading or it will just end up in the trash.

Send them copies of articles you have written. If you haven't written any articles, then write some! Never underestimate the power of your knowledge. Put it on paper and share it with your clients and your industry. Invite them to attend or send them a summary of workshops you have given. Volunteer to be interviewed by newspapers and organizations, and make this public.

For those who are targeting the residential market, get on the phone. Most Sunday newspapers have a home section. Every season, the newspapers have large special-interest sections on getting ready for spring. They include articles on spring-cleaning, home remodeling, flower gardening, and so on. These reporters need stories. Why not be the authority in your area and offer these writers your expertise and advice in an interview. Chances are your offer will be graciously accepted.

Do your homework. Make sure the information you provide is correct. Be the authority. Don't confuse opinions or theories with facts. Reporters are not experts in your industry so they will believe anything. A well-informed reader could challenge your statements and prove you wrong.

This would turn a powerful form of free advertising and credibility into a booby trap! Never try to fake it. Be sincere, and if you don't have the answer, be honest and then find the answer.

(Now get on the phone!)

How to Be a Friend to Your Customers

Do you contact your friends only when you need something? Regular contact with your customers will drastically increase your sales and your credibility. If you build relationships founded on trust and integrity, you will have a customer base that is conducive to resales, cross sales and up sales. Otherwise your growth will become a constant battle of finding new clients, which is very expensive, and often a continuous headache.

Don't wait on your customers to return to you; you go to them. Use any excuse to maintain friendly contact with your client base. Whenever you provide a product or service, make a follow-up phone call or write a thank you card within two days of the transaction.

Customers often experience "buyer's remorse." You have to make certain they are glad to have done business with you. Make sure they know you appreciate their business and you are always available if they have any concerns or questions. Tell them to call you personally if they have any problems. Also, let them know that you are proud of the way the job turned out. If you are not proud, do whatever you need to do to get that way!

Write personalized letters to the customer later on in the year to assure they are still thrilled with your product or service. Let them know you care and they are valuable to you. Let them know you have a personal interest in their satisfaction. Make them feel special!

If you run specials, let your existing client base in on the secret first. Make sure they get preferential treatment. Give them the best prices, deals and guarantees you can afford to give. Whatever the reason, stay in touch with your customer!

How to Target Your Market

K now who your prospects are. Aim, focus on your target audience, and focus again. If you chase two rabbits at the same time, they will both get away. It is extremely difficult to market more than one prospective category at a time.

For instance, both residential and commercial simultaneously should not be targeted in the same manner. Their needs and desires are too extreme. Business owners are looking at a return on investment. "How much money will I make from your product or service? I don't want to give you this big stack of money unless I am going to get a bigger stack." Residential or homeowners, on the other hand, may also be looking for an investment. However, this market requires a more personal touch.

For example, if your service or product is focused on their house, it may be a house to you, but it is their "home." Home is a sanctuary, a retreat from the outside world, a very personal and private part of their lives. The marketing mentality must also be personal.

A scenario to help you understand the extreme difference is in order. We will take a mistake and place it on a commercial jobsite. We will then take the same EXACT mistake and place it on a homeowner's job.

I love to tell this story. You folks who have heard me before, get over it. You liked it the first time you heard it!

"The great mistake." You are cleaning the exterior of a house for a building contractor. Everything is going great and it's a beautiful day! The birds are singing, the sun is shining, and you are spraying water and making money. You turn the corner of the house and give your hose a big pull. "SNAP" goes the rose bush. "Aw, shucks, that's going to cost me 20 bucks!" No big deal, right? Most folks would just have the contractor take it out of their pay. Done deal. No big deal.

My advice to turn this mistake into a pat on the back would be to go purchase an identical rose bush and plant it. I would then tell the contractor about the mistake and that I had completely taken care of it. Now I have not placed the responsibility of my mistake on the contractor. He doesn't have to make a half-dozen calls and baby-sit a landscaper and I am a hero. I just bought customer loyalty for 20 bucks. Being honest is good, but going the extra mile and taking care of my entire mistake is major marketing.

OK, same story. You are cleaning the exterior of a

home for a homeowner. Everything is going great and it's a beautiful day! The birds are singing, the sun is shining, yada, yada, yada. "SNAP" goes the rosebush! Being the honest person you are, you ring the doorbell and before you can speak of the loathsome deed, the homeowner bursts into tears with face in hands. You are at the scene as you comfort her (or him) with a wonderful smile and say, "Don't worry about that. I'll just go buy you another one and have it planted in a jiffy."

With tears streaming, the homeowner cries, "But you can't buy another one like that. Aunt Edna gave me that rose bush three years ago and she just died last September!"

Some things money just can't buy. Some mistakes just cannot be reversed, especially when you are working around

> "There is No Right Way to Do the Wrong Thing."

homes and personal lives. So keep that in mind as you target your homeowner market. Your strategies must be personal.

Once the first step in targeting your market has been taken and the decision to target one or the other has been made, you can fine-tune your sights even more. For instance, pretend you are targeting homeowners. Ask yourself where you might find these individuals in great numbers. Would coupons on the reverse side of grocery store receipts hit your homeowner target? You know, you go to the grocery store and buy $200 worth of potato chips and sodas and the back of the receipt has 20 coupons…one from Subway, a two-for-one at Burger King, and a special on carpet cleaning – any two rooms for $35.

Would this advertising plan hit your target market? Yes it would, but very sparingly. Homeowners do shop for groceries, but then so do apartment dwellers, home renters, college students, mobile home renters, and others. In fact, most people who buy groceries do not own their home. If only one person out of 10 could even have a possible need for your service, you are completely wasting 90 percent of your advertising bang.

What if you contact a homeowners' association and give a 10-minute talk to the membership on the benefits and money-saving advantages of using your service? What percent of this plan would hit your targeted market? 100 percent! KABOOM!

If you feel uneasy about a presentation, just pass out information on how your products and services will benefit them. Then make it a priority to get involved with a group that will help you in your presentation skills. Toastmasters International has many clubs in nearly every city. In my opinion, this should be one of the first steps to give you knowledge and confidence in public speaking.

By getting into the homeowners' association, you have hit your target precisely and those with the need are most likely going to use your company. If you want a couple of good salespeople, approach the assciation president and vice president and tell them if they each get you 10 sales you will perform their services for free. To convey a sense of urgency, you could also offer to the general membership that the first 10 contracts receive a 20 percent price reduction, free gift or additional service. Any way you see this, you are looking at approximately 30 sales, depending on the size of the association. If your product or service averages $325, that is a whopping $9,750!

Don't overlook or discount the word-of-mouth sales from referrals you will receive from your satisfied clients. When your clients see and believe you treat their home as sacred and you truly care, they will want you to succeed and go to great lengths to help you! Why? Because, again, their home is personal, so they take your actions personal. What is the cost of this marketing tactic? If you choose the presentation – NADA! If you choose the printing, ah…the cost of the printing.

MAKE MARKETING A BALANCE

To those who have heard me speak or write on this subject before, I ask you to bear with me; however, I would like to point out that repetition is the mother of learning.

We cannot depend on one source of advertising. Marketing will be a balance of all your advertising efforts. When grandma made those biscuits, she used lots of different ingredients. One of those ingredients

"Don't Wait for Your Ship to Come in. Swim Out to It."

was lard. Have you ever just taken a spoonful of lard and gobbled it up? YUCK! How about a mouthful of flour? A tablespoon of salt with a buttermilk chaser? GROSS! But boy, let grandma put them together and you have some breakfast!

Just like it takes a balance of ingredients to make those biscuits, you cannot depend solely on any one source or ingredient for your marketing recipe. So, where should you spend your advertising dollars? TV, radio, newspapers, magazines, classifieds, direct mail, flyers, press releases, personalized pens, trade shows, phone books, billboards, movie theater ads, community service programs? We could run out of ink listing them all, but not before you run out of money!

You have to develop a marketing plan and a budget, then stick to it. The one constant in all of your marketing efforts and theme has to be credibility. Now that you may be getting a hint of the magic of marketing, let's look at what the media wants and a few marketing strategies.

Chapter 4

What Does the Media Want You to Do?

W hat are the objectives of the media salespeople? Media sales reps are trained to sell *their* inventory, not your inventory. An unfortunate demand that is put on the media salesperson is that their owners and managers make them focus on building a month as opposed to a career. "Write business, hit budget this month, sell those spots now!"

Most media reps are trained only to discuss rates, ratings, promotions, formats, color, locations, placements and going to lunch. From my experience, most media groups are not familiar with the real issues of advertising. Nor do they ask the key questions vital to a business. When and if you find a media sales rep with the magic, treasure him or her as a sacred source of information.

More than 90 percent of the businesses that advertise with a local medium are not happy with their results. Advertisers are not happy with their advice, copy and schedules of their local media reps. The turnover in clients and salespeople in this arena is appalling. I would bet that over 60 percent of advertisers that were advertising in or on a particular medium

12 months ago are not doing so now. It would also be a safe bet that salespeople that called on small and medium-sized advertisers 18 months ago are now gone.

As for your local advertisers, the best chance you have is to learn. There are few experts that reside there. Learn all you can about each medium. Learn how to schedule your ads and how to write your own copy. If you don't manage your own advertising or find someone who can, you will not find much success in your local advertising efforts.

HOW TO USE TV, RADIO AND MAGAZINES

These are all extremely effective; however, TV and radio can be very costly. If you do your homework, the return can be phenomenal!

When any of these tactics are used, targeting your market should certainly not be left to chance. You should know everything possible about your target. What do they eat, drink, read, watch, listen to, play, buy, drive, want, wear, shop, need, dream and have?

This can be used for your target market, no matter what form of marketing you choose. This could be the beginning of your marketing plan. Fill in the blanks:

What do they…

_____Eat
_____Drink
_____Play
_____Work
_____Read
_____Listen to

_____Buy

_____Drive

_____Shop

Once you have filled in the blanks, go back to each item and answer the question "where." Where do they eat, drink, play, etc.

Remember: It doesn't matter what you or I like. It only matters what the customer likes!

Leave no detail unknown. KNOW your prospect. Where do they work, live, vacation, dine, and spend their spare time? What are their interests, hobbies, pastimes, sports, likes, dislikes, political views, religious preferences? Dig deep and leave no stone unturned.

It does not matter what you like. It only matters what the prospect likes.

If only part of the above information is known, it can be priceless. If we know our prospects are homeowners in their sixties-to-mid-seventies, would we want to run a $700, 30-second spot on Saturday Night Live at 11:30 PM? NO!

The same holds true for magazines – think before you advertise. Magazines are so specialized today, you can reach a targeted audience in the center of the bull's eye at a fraction of the cost of other methods. If you are selling shovels with a kickstand, I am sure there is a specialized magazine that only landscape contractors receive, and the kickstand shovels would sell.

Radio and TV generally draw in the big bucks with two sales features: frequency and reach. If one is operating a home-based business and prefers not to travel to distant lands, frequency would be most important. Frequency, of course, is how many times your "spot" or commercial is broadcast at a given time.

A quick word to those that are hurriedly reading through this section because you have already determined that TV and radio are not for you. My experience with companies that make this decision so quickly is this: FEAR. They have fear. Fear of the money, fear of the risk, fear of the unknown, and sometimes even fear that it might work.

Often businesses or people are limited by their own beliefs. If you cannot see yourself as a success, it will not happen. If you cannot imagine your phones ringing with so much work you have to grow, it will not happen! If you limit your success in your own mind, you are already defeated.

You are at least trapped in a financial position that you have chosen. I challenge you to put forth effort and look beyond the limitations you have put on yourself. I guarantee if you don't try to become a millionaire in this industry, you will not. On the other hand, if you open your eyes to the opportunities and possibilities that lie before you, you may very well see yourself in a new light.

Often we find ourselves living within the boundaries of life that others have set for us. We do not have to live our lives in the same manner as we have. We can reach beyond those individual limits. We can take down the old picture we have of ourselves in our minds. Put up the new picture, the picture of you as a success. The picture that has no limitations and is already a success!

You Must Have Frequency

Don't ever expect to run one ad and have the phones ring off the hook. While this occasionally happens, it is not wise to expect it. This is the beginning of gaining credibility.

All marketing takes persistence and just a few ads usually will not do it. Commit to a marketing strategy and see it through. The first time a prospect sees your ad, it will hardly get their attention unless they have an immediate need. Once you are part of their TV, radio or magazine lives, you then will earn their trust, then their business. Consistency in advertising establishes stability, credibility and success to the public.

Tons of businesses waste thousands of dollars airing TV spots and magazine ads, and after six or seven spots they jump ship. If only they would have stuck it out one more month, they could witness the real power of persistence and have prospered. However, this is not the magic; this is work!

The magic isn't something you can buy. The magic comes after the work. Don't be too quick to jump ship! If you advertise…they will come. The Magic will keep them there.

What is Reach and How Important Is It?

Reach is the other feature that is driven hard to you by your radio and TV salespeople as so significant, and it may be. However, if you operate a home security system business, why would you want your ad to reach folks 200 miles away?

Keep in mind that a far reach is also a far reach into your pocketbook! The media charges dearly for the ability to air their programming great distances. Case and point: I was on vacation in Jamaica. I sought the refuge of my hotel room after a long afternoon on the beach. I flopped down on the bed with my energy drained from the day's burning sun. All my troubles and worries were miles away across the ocean, back in the Carolinas.

I clicked on the TV set and behold, there was my bearded mug saying "at HydroTech, our goal is to exceed your expectations." I kid you not. We may have been famous on the island, but we never received one call from Jamaica and I am sure I would have remembered if any of our technicians did a job there.

Reach in some markets may be important. Chances are a 20-mile radius of your office or home could keep you busy until retirement. Keep your money where it works.

WHAT ABOUT CABLE TV?

Cable offers something for everyone and is very affordable. Some channels, like the real estate channel, are as cheap as $300 a month and your message will air as often as once per hour!

Let's look at some of the programming that would be ideal and has proven to work in the pressure cleaning industry. Homeowners that use our services tend to be tuned into programs that offer helpful information on home improvements and gardening. You will hit your target with this programming.

How many college students watch programs on faux painting their dining room or developing the perfect soil for Japanese maples? The sports and news channels also work very well. The well-informed tend to be more interested in quality and safety as opposed to price.

Homeowners over 65 are good targets because they often own their home. (No payments.) They sometimes have good retirement benefits and a hefty nest egg. This audience has a need for your service and often doesn't want to or cannot do the work themselves. They want good work and no surprises. They are usually willing to pay a fair price.

When choosing ads on cable, constantly be aware of what your target will be viewing. Cable TV offers a short reach but the frequency is active and the cost is reasonable. Start your own in-house ad agency. Ad agencies often get a 15 percent discount on radio and TV spots. This is standard industry practice and YOU are entitled to if you are doing the work.

MAGAZINES WILL HIT YOUR TARGET

Another word concerning magazine ads is in order. Don't discount the power of magazines. This vehicle will hit the nail on the head. If you are in the market to buy or sell a home, you probably will purchase a local real estate magazine. This is the perfect place for an exterior

cleaning company to advertise. There is nothing a homeowner can do to improve their street appeal more for the money than to clean it thoroughly! Nothing! It will sell faster and appraise higher.

When you utilize magazines, make sure you take full advantage of the power of photos. Use a picture of an incredibly dirty house. Then take an after picture. The text beneath could read something like this: "Which would you want to call home?"

Tip: Pictures are powerful. In the pressure cleaning arena, you should always have a camera at your disposal. You NEVER know when the picture that will sell a number of high-dollar jobs will make itself available.

When choosing a magazine as your advertising vehicle, do your homework. What does your target read? Magazines WILL hit your target. Fleet trucks, aviation, high rise, office buildings, historical restoration, government contacts, restaurant owners, shopping center owners, property managers, heavy equipment operators, car dealerships, builders, hospital maintenance, car enthusiasts, restoration and remodeling specialists, paint contractors, masonry contractors, senior citizens…and the list goes on. There is a magazine for everyone! The price is right and the target is NAILED!

How to Create Ad Scripts

Ordinarily, my advice is to let the professionals develop a commercial for you that would win awards. Why not? They are the experts; this is what they get paid to do!

Pressure cleaning is not an ordinary business. Most writers and creators don't have a clue to the complexity and processes that the professional pressure cleaner employs. They are just like everyone else; they don't know where to start on a professional script.

No one knows your business like you know your business. If the ad people are confident in their abilities, give them a 30-minute infomercial on what makes you different.

Always proof your material before it is placed on the air. A radio station had a commercial made for us and it aired while I was on vacation. The spot was not too bad, other than the announcer said, "Never paint your home!" I had left word for the spot to convey that with a HydroTech house wash, many times your home will not need repainting. Its mildewed and dirty condition just gave the appearance of a home in need of paint. Four small words – "never paint your home" – could have made HydroTech a lot of enemies in the paint contracting community. Many have stated, "But Steve, that was just a mistake. Nobody would believe that." I urge you to never underestimate the power of the media!

Yes, people will deceive. Play it safe. It is your reputation. Read and have others proof your scripts. Once it is on the airways, it's literally in stone.

Keep an eye and ear out for words that make the public uneasy. In my opinion, "powerwash" is a good word to avoid since it could convey to a prospect use of high pressure water with possibilities of ripping wood, damaging paint, and intruding water through windows and attics. Doesn't a soft, gentle spray that rinses away the dirt and grime sound much more appealing? (Back to the homeowner mode of marketing: it is personal.") If you are not using a soft, gentle spray, I certainly recommend using the process.

Now, if your company name incorporates the word "powerwash," don't worry. If you have a business with momentum and an honorable reputation, keep the name and guard it with you life! If you are just getting started though, I would recommend a more user-friendly name.

Just say no to the word "chemicals." In today's search for the environmentally minded, you can be the answer! Use detergents, solutions, soaps, or even cleaners. Chemicals are what they use to kill insects, weeds, and rodents. Let's not even allow this word in our residential vocabulary.

Examine your processes in detail. What sets you apart from your competition? It can be something as small as using pH meters around a home's grounds to guarantee undisturbed pH levels or by performing exterior inspections to aid in preventative maintenance. A system where every single job is quality controlled by the owner or a supervisor is a service that would set you apart from your competition. Another perk could be an unconditional money-back guarantee.

For your review, I have included a few radio scripts that have proven successful for us in the past. If you have purchased this book, all I need is a request from your company to use or modify these scripts. I hope that all the work that went into these spots will bring forth all of the rewards and profits for you that they did for us. Have fun!

Radio Scripts That Have Worked

This spot was aired on a talk radio station. We got a pretty good response, but talk radio tends to draw price shoppers.

MAURY: Steve Stephens with HydroTech Pressure Cleaning Technologies is here. HydroTech is a small pressure cleaning company in Raleigh, yet you have HydroTech certified companies all over the U.S.

STEVE: That's right, Maury. We have the most elite nationally recognized training facility in the world. Companies fly into Raleigh, take our courses, and return to their cities better educated to serve their customers.

MAURY: Wait a minute. A course to wash a house?

STEVE: Sure, but that's just one of many.

MAURY: A power washer, a jug of bleach and some high pressure, right?

STEVE: No way! You don't need a course to ruin people's property!

MAURY: I'm sure many homeowners have had damage done to their homes by untrained hands. What's the secret to HydroTech?

STEVE: In a nutshell, it's a soft gentle spray, using solutions that delicately penetrate into the pores of the paint. That's where the spores of the mildew thrive. A trained, certified technician can educate the homeowner in preventative maintenance. And most of all, no bleach, no high pressure, and no harsh chemicals.

MAURY: Call HydroTech for a free brochure and to schedule a HydroTech soft wash. 876-3320. Or visit their website, www. hydrotechnc.com.

HYDROTECH (PHONE CALL TO MOM) This spot was aired on a jazz station and a soft rock station. Good response. Women are good targets. They are often willing to be educated, they care for their property, and usually don't mind a higher price for peace of mind.

(PHONE RINGS.) Hello? Oh, hi Mom. Oh, I love our new house. Yeah, we still have so much to do, but we've really got some big plans, Mom. We're starting on the outside. Well, the first impression someone gets of our house starts on the outside, so we called HydroTech. You've heard of HydroTech? Well, I'm sure you have. HydroTech has a great reputation for quality service.

Yes, Mom. All of their cleaning products are environmentally safe. Uh-huh. They also use state-of-the-art cleaning methods instead of high pressure that can cause wear on the paint. Well, we called last week and someone from HydroTech came out right away and gave us an estimate absolutely free. And, all of their work is guaranteed and fully insured. And, if we take care of the exterior of our house, we're gonna save on major home improvement costs later on.

Sounds like I've grown up? Well, thanks Mom. Now, only if wall papering was this easy.

(Announcer): Protect your home investment. Call HydroTech today for your free estimate, 876-3320. That's 876-3320.

> "Advertising is what makes you think you longed all your life for something you've never heard of before."

This spot was really funny. The houses talked like truck drivers on the CB radio. The response was good, but phones did not ring off the hook.

HOUSE 1: Hey, check out the brick rambler at 2203. Must've got a new paint job.

HOUSE 2: Negatory, my friend. Her owner just gave her a real intense shower from HydroTech.

HOUSE 1: Hydro-who?

HOUSE 2: HydroTech. You've seen how cherry that '65 Mustang at 2207 looks, right?

HOUSE 1: Yeah! But that's a car.

HOUSE 2: Exactly. You don't think that guy paints that thing every week do you?

HOUSE 1: Nah. They use soap and water.

HOUSE 2: Uh-huh.

HOUSE 1: You mean?

HOUSE 2: Yeah.

HOUSE 1: Hey! What an idea.

HOUSE 2: That's the idea behind HydroTech. And if you've noticed, her shutters look like new. And how about her sidewalk and walkway.

HOUSE 1: Oh, clean! Hey, look at the mortar between those bricks.

HOUSE 1: Spotless, all because of HydroTech. A HydroTech soft wash is friendly to the environment.

HOUSE 1: Smart! I hope I can get my owner to use HydroTech; but alas, houses can't speak. People talk.

HOUSE 2: Don't be so sure. Have you seen the sign in her front yard?

HOUSE 1: Read it for me, will you? My picture window is a little bit milky.

HOUSE 2: It says, "Another home, HydroTech clean. Call 876-3320."

HOUSE 1: 876-3320. I've got it right up here in my attic.

This spot was SMOKIN! Women love their homes. I requested a female announcer and it came out GREAT!

(ANNOUNCER) You fell in love with that giant maple that drapes over the rooftop corner, and the winding pathway lined with azalea bushes and the spacious deck that opens up into the woods. It's your home and just like there's not a nook or cranny that you don't' know, there's probably not a spot, stain or smear that you haven't seen and wanted to get rid of.

Let HydroTech Cleaning Technologies take care of your home's exterior with state-of-the-art cleaning products, not high pressure. HydroTech uses environmentally safe cleaning products, created by their on-staff chemist. In fact, HydroTech is nationally recognized as the industry's information source. HydroTech offers a variety of home cleaning packages that won't harm paint, siding, plants or pets.

If you've been thinking about treating the deck, let HydroTech restore it to its pristine condition first, then treat it. It makes a difference. Call HydroTech today at 876-3320 and find out how an annual exterior cleaning of your home can preserve its beauty. 876-3320. HydroTech Cleaning Technologies, the only name in pressure cleaning.

How to Sell Your Home: *This one did not win awards, but it did pay for itself a few times over. This spot aired on Christian radio. The response from Christian radio is good; however, be prepared to haggle on price. We offer a ministry discount, but we do not negotiate.*

ANNOUNCER: This is "How to Sell Your Home." You're on the air. Hello? Is someone there?

HOMEOWNER: Yes, sir. We're trying to sell our home and I noticed the other day a lot of mildew, especially in the back. Well, the thing is, we had the house painted just a couple of years back and I don't think we can afford another paint job, especially when we are planning to move out. Know what I mean? Got any ideas?

ANNOUNCER: Before deciding to paint your home, get a HydroTech soft wash. HydroTech will make your home look like a million and it's quite possible that you won't even need a paint job.

HOMEOWNER: Well, I don't think I could do that to my flowers and landscaping. My roses have finally bloomed.

ANNOUNCER: Rest easy my friend. A HydroTech soft wash is kind to the environment and not only will your house look great, so will your driveway, your sidewalks, your gutters – at a fraction of the cost of painting your home.

HOMEOWNER: Hey! That sounds great! What's the phone number?

ANNOUNCER: Call HydroTech at 876-3320. That's 876-3320.

This was a good spot as well. We received calls for a couple of years after this aired. Make sure you always know how your customer heard about you.

ANNOUNCER: Do you paint your car every time it gets dirty? Of course not. That would be a ridiculous waste of money. So why paint your home just because it's dirty? Schedule a HydroTech exterior cleaning.

Every day your home is exposed to dirt, dust, rain and the dangerous rays of the sun. These elements create a sandpapering effect that ruins the finish. HydroTech can help you retain the beauty of your home and prolong the life of your paint and siding.

Experience the pride of a well groomed home with freshly restored sidewalks, driveways and decks. HydroTech uses mild detergents and low pressure to protect your investment. HydroTech brings chemistry and physics together and achieves superior environmentally safe results.

HydroTech ensures customer satisfaction on every job and often exceeds the customers' expectations. Call today to schedule a consultation. 876-3320. Your home. Your investment. Your peace of mind. HydroTech, unmistakably the best.

> *"To become successful, you must be a person of action. Merely to 'know' is not sufficient. It is necessary to know and do."*
> — Napoleon Hill

ANNOUNCER: Image is everything. If negative, it can be difficult to overcome. The outside of your building will be a reflection of what is going on inside. Have you looked lately? First impressions are only made once. HydroTech Cleaning Technologies is cleaning up the Carolinas.

City life surrounds a building. The public, tenants, and important clients all interact with your building. Our goal is to restore their outer surfaces to their maximum shine and enhance the profile of your facility.

HydroTech remains environmentally responsible in our community. Harnessing the dynamic power of hot water for cleaning enables them to minimize the use of harsh chemicals. Our high flow, high heat pressure cleaning equipment uses an oscillating turbo tip rotary action. This removes the pollution that clings to your building, curbs and sidewalks without damaging its surface.

Maintain your real estate investment. Let your image speak to the community. HydroTech will breathe new life into a tired looking facility. HydroTech is cleaning up the Carolinas.

Do I Need the Phone Book?

You may be an incredible professional basketball player. You may have the talents, skills and gifts that could make you millions. The bottom line is if you are not in the game, then people don't know you are a player. So it is with the phone book.

This is not an option for a new business. If you are in business to prosper for the long run, this will set you apart from the "wannabes." When prospects need your product or service, they look for YOU in THE phone book, not a competitor of the phone book.

I am not here to endorse "the Real Yellow Pages." In fact, we have somewhat of a love/hate relationship. Mostly hate, because from my experience, long-term relationships are not important to them. However, I must be honest with you in saying that the phone book works. I believe they could use a good course in customer service.

Our first ad was a very modest ad for $150 a month. At the time, it seemed like a fortune to me and was a very large step in my business commitment. The first month, we received enough business from this one source to pay for the entire year's bill!

The next year, the cost went up about 25 percent. I was given the option to increase the size of my ad, and I would only be charged the extra 25 percent. Not much of an option, is it? Either increase your size and pay more, OR keep the same small ad and pay more. Although I felt a little uncomfortable, I knew it was a good investment and took the increase.

The next year, guess what happened? The rates went up again. Yes, another 25 percent. Or I could increase my ad size to the next level and only pay the additional 25 percent. As

> ## "The Shortest Way to do Many Things Is to Do One Thing at a Time."
> — *Samuel Smiles (1812-1904)*
> *Physician & Writer*

expected, the second year's ad paid for itself in about three months. The next few years, the same ritual occurred and I got angrier each year, feeling violated and resentful. I put someone else in charge of handling the phone book because of the bad taste I had for them. Our business prospered as I spent more time working on the future of our company and less on the day-to-day operations.

The same ritual went on for many years until I asked someone on our office how much we had in the budget for the phone book. ONE-THOUSAND, FOUR-HUNDRED AND FIFTY DOLLARS a month is what we were paying! That is SEVENTEEN THOUSAND FOUR-HUNDRED DOLLARS a year! I thought we had lost our mind, but it was my fault for running from the problem.

I attempted to negotiate our cost since I knew other businesses that had the same size ad as ours were paying half the cost. It turned out the other businesses were newer customers and had started off with larger ads in their phone-book journey. We cancelled our ad the next year. The phone company then offered a "new customer" discount just as they did my first year. I accepted their offer.

The next year, guess what happened? That's right. They had an increase, or I could increase to the next size. I cancelled again that year.

> ## "If you want the rainbow, you have to put up with the rain."
> — *Dolly Parton*

Our company now has momentum and is well known in our community. We now run a year in the book, then a year out and take their discount. We cannot tell by our sales if the ad is running or not. People still say they got our name out of the phone book, even when we are not advertising. I believe that many people hold on to the same book for a couple of years. That's why they still call. I am not sure about that; it is just a guess.

My best advice on this subject is to stay on top. DON'T get too busy to take care of the phone book. Always ask your calling prospects how they hear about you. This is a fantastic icebreaker for conversation and is vital for your marketing records. I really feel the phone book is a necessity the first five to eight years. If you can get a good representative that takes care of you, then I would use it indefinitely. Only your own records will show you exactly what is working. An ad does not have to be the largest, but it does need to read credibility and professionalism. After a few years, the magic could make the need for the phone book disappear!

I recommend studying the phone book ads for your business from other companyies' ads. Remember to check out ads when you travel out of your state. Play with them and take the best from the best. Then write your own, improving upon what everyone else has done.

Bigger is not always better when you have the "magic."

(irect ‖ ail

Direct mail is an absolute gold mine, only if it hits your target consistently. Five-thousand dollars ago we were promised thousands of beautiful full-color postcards to be delivered to exclusive homes in excess of $300,000. Our office received one call from a mobile homeowner. The cards were beautiful and very professionally put together. I was very proud of them. The sad thing is, we've only been able to use them as examples of good design and bad mailing list choices.

I remember another mailing list we purchased and spent over $7,000 in just the brochure printing costs. You can imagine the cost of postage alone. When we did not receive a single response, I got concerned! The brochures were to saturate all painting contractors in the Eastern United States. I contacted the mailing list people and they assured me they went out with verification from the postal service. I asked how they obtained our list. After way too much conversation, I finally found out their big secret was the phone book.

I then hired a few telemarketers to follow up by calling

hundreds of our targets. We, too, got our leads from the phone book – the phone book with all the Yellow Page listings in the United States.

You would think after three nights of calling our prospects, one would have received our costly brochure. Not one painting contractor received our brochure on an "add-on" business. The brochures must have been captured and abducted by aliens from outer space. Or maybe they are in that secret place where the dryer puts all my socks that it eats.

Check the references and destination of your costly mailers. Technology is so advanced that you can actually get a list of all single females that use a notebook computer only on Fridays and drive a BMW. This tactic works well if your target really is the recipient. Look for the "magic" in those with whom you do business.

Some of the best direct mailers are the ones we have done on our own. You can get copies of real estate records at your local courthouse or register of deeds. One way we use this is in our cedar roof prospecting. The records can actually be bought electronically.

NOTE: When any of us see a cedar roof that needs restoring and preserving, we just write down the address. We can then just enter in the address on the computer, and presto! There is the homeowner's first and last name, address, when they bought the home, how much it cost and the tax value. This is more information than I need to know; however, now we can send a personalized letter to the homeowners and educate them on wood technology.

At times you could just ride around forever and write down addresses for roofs, decks, drives, and send them prices as well. Many times when they call and you have already given them a price, they just schedule the work. I have a few different letters that have worked well for us. Check these out and I hope you find some you can use. Take note of to whom the letters are addressed. Examples include homeowners for exterior house cleaning and cedar roof restoration, and property managers for shopping centers. There are also some for new construction cleaning and high rise buildings, and so on. Have fun and make some money! But remember the magic!

MODEL LETTERS THAT HAVE WORKED

Now let's take a look at some real examples of letters that have worked for me and others.

This thick cardstock mailer is an inexpensive way to introduce your company to your prospective clients. Notice how Pressure Cleaning Technologies was able to show homeowners the many different services they provide. If offering discounts, I suggest giving a price first. Then have the customer present the coupon.

This letter has worked well for years It usually gets a foot in the door and sometimes eliminates the price shoppers.

Dear Mr. Builder,

It is an absolute pleasure to be writing you regarding all of your pressure cleaning needs. Our company is here to provide you with safe, proper pressure cleaning solutions.

We do not incorporate technicians with "one chemical cleans all" mentalities. Our company has been formally trained and certified on the special needs of new construction. We are educated on the composition of different types of brick. We understand the sensitivity of the many types of brick, including soft face and sandy face brick. Our goal is to exceed your expectations.

Your time is valuable. You shouldn't have to concern yourself with a pressure-cleaning contractor whom you have to babysit. Do you find yourself worrying about water on hardwoods, tarnished fixtures, burnt or blown-out mortar joints or foundation vents? If so, we are the answer to your problem.

Our company uses environmentally safe products that are strong enough to accomplish the job, yet mild enough to protect your investment. Ever lost any landscaping due to harsh chemicals? We use neutralizing agents to maintain your soil at its proper pH level so your landscaping will remain beautiful and flourish!

As we perform our services, the technician's eyes are always open for opportunities to make you look good. We incorporate packages developed exclusively for the needs of new home contractors. This eliminates any surprises and hidden costs. This also makes your job easy in scheduling and proves an almost foolproof communications system.

We are very eager to become a part of your team. Thank you so much for your time. We look forward to another satisfied client.

With much anticipation!

Sincerely,

Steve Stephens

The next letter is one that I use only on referrals. This letter is extremely personal and effective. Before using this letter as a model, I would consider seriously whom it is being sent to and whom the referral is from. It certainly is not for direct mail, but I thought it could be useful. If you have done business for 10 years and have only one account that you feel this way about, TREASURE IT AND KEEP IT! Then, since we tend to be LIKE those we associate with, ask for them to refer you to someone. Chances are you will pick up another winning account.

Dear Mr. Reid,

It is an absolute pleasure to be writing you in regards to all of your pressure cleaning needs. My name is Steve Stephens, founder of HydroTech Cleaning Technologies. I am presently searching for one, possibly two, large residential new-construction accounts.

I have learned that success is usually a byproduct of integrity, character, honesty and consistency. I also believe you can tell a lot about a company or person by their peers, and the company that they keep. That is why I am contacting you. I asked Steve Miller if he knew of anyone that could possibly use our services. His first response was you. His opinion, Byron, is extremely important to me. I believe Steve incorporates the qualities I listed above; therefore, I can only assume your values are similar, if not the same.

The list of "features and benefits" of using HydroTech is long. Our primary focus is to make you look good to your superiors and public, make the job happen, and to bring you solutions, not problems. HydroTech, without exception, is the industry's information source. We have been featured on the covers of the international trade magazines, *Cleaner Times* and *Pressure Concepts*. I am a contributing author of *The Power Washer's Guidebook*, selling internationally. I am on the Board of

Directors of PWNA (Power Washers of North America) and I am the chairman of the Technical Support Network. This is a problem-solving committee for pressure cleaning contractors all over America. I also conduct monthly courses and seminars throughout the United States for pressure cleaning contractors to improve their businesses and actually become licensed and "HydroTech Certified."

I tell you this, Byron, not to impress you, but to impress upon you the lengths HydroTech goes to be unique and to assure our clients have the best quality product and service our industry has to offer. We value our clients and strive to exceed their expectations. I would truly value the opportunity to meet you and become a part of your team. David Weekley Homes will be good for our image...HydroTech will be good for yours.

With much appreciation,

Steve

This next letter is one we include in many of our highrise projects. It has proven to be effective when we have needed it. You will notice there are many phrases I repeat in a number of different letters and ads. This is an example of finding something good and keeping it.

Many of the phrases in our industry can be used in a number of different applications. For instance, the phrase "Your company name is good for our image...HydroTech is good for yours," has proven to be catchy and it also builds up the client. I have had several prospects comment on that closing phrase and become residual clients afterward. I would only use this phrase if I were truly proud to be associated with the client. Go for the good accounts!

Don't be intimidated by anyone. Someone has to be doing the work; it may as well be you!

This is a cover letter for a highrise proposal. It should not be used as a direct mail piece. However, when the need arises, it could help you get the job.

Dear Frank:

Thank you very much for taking your time to help us get familiar with your property. Within this binder is the prepared estimate that you requested. Our figures were calculated after three (3) complete and detailed site surveys of your building. I would like for you to know and rest assured that HydroTech is completely prepared, equipped and focused on high-rise projects such as yours. I know you are aware of the danger of injury or death and the liability of such a project, which is why we are totally committed to: First, the safety of our employees; Second, the environment; and Third, that you receive the utmost quality our industry has to offer.

HydroTech allows only certified technicians with experience to perform our cleaning and restorations. Our company is fully insured and abides by a strict safety program set forth by us, which exceeds standard OSHA regulations. We are not a franchise; however, we do conduct seminars and training sessions, as well as provide consultations to high rise restoration contractors all over the United States.

I urge you to consider HydroTech for this project. Once again, we are focused on safety, the environment and quality. We know what it takes to safely and effectively complete this project with as little disruption to your business as possible. Grubb Management would be good for our image…HydroTech would be good for yours.

Sincerely,

Steve Stephens

This letter has resulted in many residual accounts from the shopping center market, office buildings and other rental properties. This one has been used both by direct mail to property managers as well as an e-mail. If you use this one, BE READY TO DELIVER!

Dear

We make you look good! We keep your tenants happy! We help your occupancy rate soar! Your property's image will vastly improve literally overnight, on time, on budget, and with no disruption to your tenants' business.

It is an absolute pleasure to introduce you to HydroTech Pressure Cleaning Technologies. We have been a part of this community for over 25 years and we are now focusing our efforts on upgrading the image of the Triangle's properties. We are not a typical pressure cleaning company. We are able to harness over 200 degrees of hot water along with the proper chemicals to annihilate just about any stain. Our state-of-the-art cleaning processes are chosen dependent upon the molecular structure of the stain. Our technicians are nationally certified and holds a valid license numbers and we incorporate an on-staff chemist with a master's from NCSU.

When you entrust your projects, reputation and image to us, we are committed, dedicated and driven to make you look good and make the job happen! We will provide you with the most up-to-date and most professional service our industry has to offer. We are the nation's information source and are eager to prove to you what we have proven to the rest of the nation. I sincerely urge you to give us a try. We are eager to be a part of your team so you can experience the quality, peace of mind and confidence our services will bring to your life.

Sincerely,

Steve Stephens

A Proposal Template

We include this letter, or a variation of this letter, in all of our roof restoration proposals. This is not for direct mail, yet since our industry is so specialized, I thought I would include a complete proposal for you as a template, if needed.

Presented To:
Suzanne Johnson

Presented by: Steve Stephens

Dear Suzanne,

Thank you so much for giving us the opportunity to assist you in the restoration and preservation of your cedar roof. Enclosed is the estimate we prepared for you. Our numbers were calculated after a complete and detailed site survey of your home. I would like for you to know HydroTech is completely prepared, equipped, and focused on projects such as yours. It is our sincere desire to provide to you the best service our industry has to offer.

HydroTech has been in business for many years, educating contract cleaners all over the nation as well as supplying our customers with the highest quality and the most reliable service possible. Our expertise and experience allow us to choose, with confidence, solutions that are powerful enough to accomplish the job, yet mild enough to protect your investment. We bring chemistry and physics together to achieve superior environmentally safe results.

HydroTech is the nation's foremost authority in cedar wood restoration and preservation. Not only will we save you thousands of dollars in costly replacement, we can actually restore and preserve roofs to provide many years of lasting beauty. In fact with proper care, cedar shakes can actually last a lifetime.

Enclosed is a partial listing of references, along with a brief description of our own wood restoration process. This is not to be confused with "powerwashing," but a true restoration. When we perform our services for you, I will make certain that your wood is restored and protected with the best possible products and processes our industry has to offer.

Thank you again for your consideration and we look forward to another satisfied client!

Thank you,

Steve Stephens

Presented To:
Suzanne Johnson
4602 Whitfield Rd
Chapel Hill, NC 27514

This proposal is all-inclusive of labor and materials as follows:

Cedar Roof Restoration	$3300
Cedar Roof Preservation	$3300
Total Turnkey Price	$6600
House Exterior Clean (Mildew & Fungus Removal)	$ 375*

Weather permitting, we should have your home completed in five workdays.

*No charge if cedar roof restoration is performed by HydroTech

This letter is not for mailing, but it is good to cover yourself if you feel that something might come back to haunt you. This letter was written primarily to bring out the fact that damage had already taken place on canopies we were to restore. If I had not WRITTEN it down, it may have been a focal point to hold our money. I've been there and thought you might appreciate a heads up!

Dear Doug,

Here is our proposal for the Tower Shopping Center awnings. These numbers were calculated by several detailed surveys of the property as well as the large test spot approved by you. The services we will perform will be a detailed restoration. We had experts from Florida to California as well as our own chemist working on solutions to the Tower problem and are now ready to begin. There are a few things I would like to note; however, I know you are aware of the conditions:

1. The burgundy/red areas are cracking and peeling and have not shown a significant change. (The Ultra Gloss Sealer may bring a positive change to their appearance.)

2. There are many "pressure washing marks" due to improper cleaning attempts. We may be able to remove these marks; however, mostly we just want you to be aware of their presence. Our process is soft and gentle and will not damage your property.

3. The price includes an Ultra Gloss Sealer, which is made of a waterproof polymer resin and is designed for LONG TERM PROTECTION. This product establishes a microscopic, non-stick chemical barrier on the awning's surface. This barrier is resistant to weather and pollutants and reduces UV damage to the material. This also makes the vinyl cleanable without a restoration.

4. Our previous price before our test panel totaled $31,000.

TOTAL TURNKEY PRICE	$25,000
LESS 14% IF PAID IN 5 DAYS	$ 3,500
TOTAL	$21,500

Thank you for considering HydroTech!

Sincerely,
Steve Stephens

> "The moment you commit and quit holding back, all sorts of unforeseen incidents, meetings, and material assistance will rise up to help you. The simple act of commitment is a powerful magnet for help.
> — *Napoleon Hill (1883 – 1970)*

Rarely do we give a proposal or written contract to a homeowner other than cedar roof projects. However, when the customer is asking for multiple services that could be confusing, it is safe to write it down. Everybody understands BEFORE work starts and emotions get in the way.

Dear Sylvia,

Thank you so much for giving us the opportunity to assist you in the restoration and cleaning of your home and decks. We are looking forward to working with you on restoring and preserving the areas outlined below. It is our sincere desire to provide to you the best service our industry has to offer.

In our experience with wood restorations, preservations and staining, we have found that the durability of stains and preservatives depends greatly on how the surface is prepped. Unfortunately, many paint contractors and pressure cleaning companies just come out and either spray bleach on the wood or just power wash it; however, at HydroTech we use a low pressure process which enables us to remove all dead wood cells and completely destroy all non-vascular plant growth.

Our expertise and experience allow us to choose, with confidence, solutions that are powerful enough to accomplish the job, yet mild enough to protect your investment. We bring chemistry and physics together to achieve superior environmentally-safe results. When HydroTech completes the restoration on your decks, they will be in the best possible condition to receive a maximum sealer and preservative.

HydroTech's exterior house cleaning mildew package restores your home's beauty by removing unsightly stains. Dirt, dust, mildew, wind and rain cause a sandpapering effect, which damages the home's surface and ruins the paint. Our cleaning system removes these elements, actually prolonging the life of the paint. The solutions kill mold and mildew,

79

rather than just bleaching it out.

Enclosed is a partial listing of our references, along with a brief description of our own wood restoration process. This is not to be confused with "power washing," but a true restoration. We are looking forward to another satisfied customer.

Thank you for your trust,

Steve Stephens

PRESENTED TO:
SYLVIA ALRMAN
901 PENTLAND CT.
RALEIGH, NC 27614

This proposal is all-inclusive of labor & materials as follows:

Deck restoration (For 3 decks)	$950.50
Deck preservation (For 3 decks)	$950.50
Mildew package	$630.00*
Brick stoops/walks	$ 42.90*

*If you elect to have us perform all of the above services, the mildew package will be reduced to $395, and the brick stoop/walks will be done at no charge.

Often, the first written contact we have with a customer is delivering them a price. In this case, a short letter is in order. I know we will be the highest price, so a little preliminary justification doesn't hurt. More times than not, we are granted jobs knowing we were the most expensive. Good clients know and can sense the magic. To them, the magic is worth the cost.

Dear Frank,

Thank you for considering HydroTech for your cleaning needs. HydroTech has been in business for several years and has become a model and source of information for the national pressure cleaning industry. We are therefore able to offer our customers the highest quality and most reliable service possible. Our expertise and experience allow us to choose, with confidence, chemicals that are powerful enough to accomplish the job, yet mild enough to protect your investment.

Outlined below is our proposal for the services discussed:
Cleaning of rust streaks on front of building:
TOTAL PRICE $1050

Our proposal is all-inclusive of labor and materials. We are happy to perform these services at your convenience, including evenings and/or weekends to avoid disruption of any business operations. We will be happy to start this project the beginning of next week, starting on November 4th. Please let us know whether you prefer us to work during the day or evening hours.

Again, thank you for considering HydroTech. We are looking forward to working with you and adding your company's name to our list of satisfied customers.

Thank you,
Steve Stephens

This is a great direct mailer to homeowners. You send this to them after you have completed the work for the builder and the homeowners take residence. Just think if you only do 300 houses per year in new construction, you should expect 50 percent of the business "after the sale." That's an estimated $41,000 the next year IF you follow the business and use a mailer similar to this one!

Dear Mr. Montas,

We at HydroTech would like to extend our congratulations on your new home. M/I Homes has gone to great lengths to assure your home incorporates the highest quality and craftsmanship available today. We are honored to be a part of this team.

As proud new homeowners, it is now your responsibility to protect your investment with periodic observations of your home's exterior. Even though the quality of your paint and the detail of the tradesmanship are unsurpassed, 365 days a year your home will be exposed to dirt, wind, rain and sun. These elements create a sandpapering effect that ruins the paint and can fade your siding. There are also natural contaminants, mildew, fungus and algae that bring their own damage to the highest quality of materials. The surface also attracts man-made dirt such as auto exhaust, industrial pollution and acid rain.

Retain the beauty of your home and prolong the life of your paint and siding with an annual exterior cleaning. While this may appear to be a formidable task, our years of experience and intensive research in this field are your assurance of state-of-the-art cleaning technologies, giving you the peace of mind that your home is receiving the ultimate in care.

Again, congratulations on your wise decision to invest in

---

an M/I home. We look forward to helping you protect your investment. Make certain that you mention you are an M/I homeowner. Since M/I has ensured that your home's exterior was meticulously detailed before you moved in, it will cost you less to maintain and protect this condition on a regular basis. We look forward to the continued care and protection of your investment for years to come, just as we have from construction to the delivery of your beautiful new home!

Sincerely,

Steve Stephens

How to Upsell Your Customers

Direct mailing is one of the best returns on your advertising dollar. The target is usually hit precisely in the bull's eye. As I have said before, the most profitable and successful marketing campaigns are the ones that we conducted ourselves. No one knows your prospects like you know your prospects.

Direct mail has been most successful for us, hands down. Major corporations want as much information about their customers as possible. They ask you to send back warranty cards filled with information about you, your family and your buying habits. They make money selling this information to list companies and determine future marketing and product decisions based on your opinions.

There are many things we can learn from the corporate big boys. We have to maintain contact with our customers.

This is the only way to sell, resell or cross-sell. We cannot get information from customers we don't communicate with. Your existing customer base is your secure future. They are people in which you have already established a relationship of loyalty and trust. It is much easier to nurture an existing relationship of trust than it is to establish a new one.

Computerize your customer profiles for the purpose of database marketing. Put the information you have about your clients to use. CONTACT your customer base several times throughout the year. This action will provide you with many sales you would not have made otherwise.

Treat every job or customer as though it were a long-term relationship, not a one-time project. You can even put together a preferred customer list. You can create many reasons for staying in touch with your customers.

Make sure the customer sees the contents of your mailing piece as legitimate and motivating, not a piece of junk mail.

SAVE YOUR DECK!
With

HYDROTECH
Pressure Cleaning Technologies

CALL: 828-3883

Remember that a picture truly is worth a thousand words in this industry!

(Back to relationships.) Having a database of your treasured customers is more than a good idea. It could be the difference between making it big versus not making it at all.

How to Get Prospects to Read Your Mail

Often the mail will be the most consistent means of contacting your customers or prospects on a regular basis. The trick with prospects is getting the mail read as opposed to tossed in the trash. If you must send out "canned" or "junk looking" mail, a personal note on the outside will give you a better shot at getting it opened.

The battle is getting it opened, read, and hopefully kept. Don't send prospects or clients things they can easily identify. Make them curious. Send out about 10 or 12 pieces a year to your customer list. This is residual business (builders, property managers, fleet customers, restaurants, etc.). Make sure each time you send a piece of mail you use a different color or shape of envelope. (This is personal. It's OK to get away from your company theme here.)

We never put the name of our business on the outside. The person doesn't have a clue what's inside! The customer or prospect wants to know what is inside and whom it's from. I guarantee if you get on my mailing list, you would not throw away a single piece of my mail without opening and reading it. That's because it's real mail and not junk mail. It's the kind of mail that makes you curious and eager to open it!

If you were on my mailing list, in January you might

get a Happy New Year card with a personal message that says: "Happy New Year! I hope it is ABSOLUTELY PHENOMENAL!" In February, you might get a Valentine's Day card that says, "Hope your day is filled with so much joy you require plastic surgery to remove the smile!" No Christmas gifts are sent from our office. In my opinion, they get lost in all the confusion of everyone else trying to be special and fuzzy this one time of year. I prefer to send birthday cards instead.

Make your name a household word to your customers at least 10 times a year. When it comes time to get their house, deck, business or anything else cleaned, you will be the only person they even think of. Also, every time they hear of anyone looking for your type of service at work or at the club, they will suggest your company. Keep that mail going to your customers.

Later, we will talk about perceived value, but if you "care enough to send the very best," send Hallmark. It's the little things.

You may be thinking, "Sure. That's fine for a big business with the money to buy all those cards to do mass mailing." Take my word for it. You cannot afford not to employ this strategy. If you are mailing a personal sales letter like some in this book, consider priority mail. IT WILL GET READ. If it is a large contract that I really want, I have their proposals delivered via overnight mail, that it unless we are able to deliver them personally.

Dealing with people on an everyday basis is often challenging. Our customers are our future. We cannot let our feelings get in the way. What I mean is we cannot consider them interruptions or pains in the behind. They are the reason we are in business. If we don't realize this as a hard business fact, we may not be in business long. I'm not talking about some of the customers or prospects; I'm talking about all of the customers and prospects.

I remember reading a book in the early '80s by Joe Girard. He was in the *Guinness Book of World Records* 12 years in a row. He was known then and now as the "world's greatest salesman." I recall him talking bout the "law of 250." He explained how he went to a Catholic funeral where they gave out Mass cards with the name and picture of the departed. He asked the undertaker how he knew how many to print. The undertaker told him that after years of counting the names where people signed in, it averaged 250 people per funeral.

He sold a car to a Protestant funeral director years later and asked him how many people usually came to see a body. The director told him about 250. He was then at a wedding when he asked

> **"I think hard work is what got me here. I didn't get all the stuff I can do by sitting around. I worked hard for it. I don't think that once you get to one level you can relax. You've got to keep going and pushing to get to that next level.**
> *– Larry Bird*

the caterer what the average turnout at a wedding was. The caterer said about 250 for the bride and 250 for the groom. (Sounds like a large wedding to me.) Nevertheless, if the average person knows 250 people well enough to invite them to a wedding or to a funeral, that's a lot of people. Now we can argue that hermits don't have many friends, but a lot of people have even more!

That means that if I have one person a week that I did not treat kindly, or they do not think I treated them fairly, I am putting the noose around my own neck. In one year, there will be 13,000 people influenced by just that one person a week. The upside is that the opposite is also true!

Think about the last movie you went to see and shelled out half a mortgage to get in and the other half on popcorn, soda and milk duds. Did you tell anyone about the movie? Have you ever gone to see a movie just because a friend told you about it?

See, we cannot afford to have just one person be dissatisfied. Sure there is going to be the occasional psycho, but you try hard anyway. I know I cannot afford to get the "last word" in just because it makes me feel better. Ripping a customer's head off, especially when they are dead wrong, is easy. It takes self-control, maturity, patience and vision to bite your tongue.

Keep in mind when you turn just one away, just one with anger or rudeness, you are running an ad campaign to 250 people. Those 250 people have money in their pocket and want to give it to you.

Chapter 6

How to Advertise & Pay Only if It Works

Bird-Dogging

Joe Girard, who I mentioned in the last chapter, is known as the world's greatest salesman and made this method famous. The pictures and brochures are my idea. It is very economical and also very effective. Depending on your business or products, you can be creative.

A pressure cleaning company, for instance, could purchase a Rolodex-type picture holder that will display about 50 pictures, two at a time. Fill this with pictures of your proudest before and after shots, then buy a business card holder for about a buck and a brochure holder for a couple of dollars. When you have these three items together and stocked, they would be called ONE bird dog kit, or "kit." I recommend making several kits at one time for convenience.

You will need to get lots of pictures and lots of copies. You will need one copy of a before and one copy of an after for each kit. This is a bit time-consuming, but a fantastic job for someone with too much time on their hands, i.e., school

89

kids, mothers-in-law or receptionists that pass too much time talking to family.

Now, for placement of your kits. Brainstorm. Where are your captive audiences? Where does your target market spend time? Where are people so bored they will read the ingredients of a soft drink can? Watch men and women as they wait to get their hair cut. Isn't the stylist usually running behind? Customers will look anywhere except at others waiting. A bird dog kit in this environment is almost guaranteed to be read cover to cover and in detail. A 10-percent commission on each sale as a result of your bird dog kit in the facility can make your stylist an easy extra two- or three-hundred dollars a month. The best part is you don't pay 'til the ad pays.

Smart entrepreneurs may decide to get two stylists and have their hair cut twice a month. The sure-fire way to make this work is to maintain contact with your "bird dogs." Refer them business often. Most importantly, pay them; they earned their commission!

Other ideas of kit placements include doctor's offices, dentist offices, chiropractors, hair and nail salons, day spas, coffee shops, golf pro shops, upper-scale video stores, tanning salons that cater to women homeowners, car detail or oil change companies with waiting rooms. Think of places to set up your kits. Be creative! Improvise! Couldn't you imagine some sort of beautiful display in a color poster form in elevators?

This is a win-win strategy; everyone prospers. When you receive a project and you are just not sure it was from a bird dog or not, pay the commission. It is also important to keep your kits well stocked, neat and orderly. I recommend at least a monthly visit to restock your kits and do business with your bird dogs. Make sure you do business with your bird dogs! Send them customers often and make certain the new customers communicate that you referred them. This, of course, brings us to fusion marketing. Again, pay your commission!

FUSION MARKETING

This strategy is simple. I refer you and you refer me. Many businesses already employ this type of system through their city chamber of commerce or other associations. Fusion marketing is probably where the idea of bird-dogging originated. We employ several fusion marketing systems within our company in a variety of different divisions. A few good ideas for marketing partners are landscaping contractors, painters, real estate agents, architects and property managers. Others that would be profitable are builders, printing companies, restaurant owners, remodeling companies, historical restoration companies, brick salespeople, car and truck salespeople, waste removal companies, and as many others as you can find that incorporate the "magic."

A word of warning. This is a very powerful tool, if you are associated with a good group. However, recommend a snake and you will probably be labeled a snake. We tend to be similar to those we associate with. If in doubt of a business' integrity, DON'T refer them. It will always be a reflection on you.

In my business, I have had the privilege of witnessing a few builder friends that we work for become multi-millionaires over the last 15 years. Each builder's company has its own features and benefits; however, they all have some things in common. A few of the similarities are that they all pay in a timely manner, they are never looking for the cheapest price, they are honest, they have impeccable reputations, they are always busy building homes and most build homes from $500,000 to over several million dollars.

So often our technicians would work in one city performing a job for one of these giants of success and remark on how professional all the subcontractors were and how easy they were to work with. The next week, they performed another project in another city for a different one of these builders that I have described. The technicians are excited to tell me that they worked with literally the same subcontractors as they did on the other builder's home in the other city! "What a coincidence!" they always suggest in delight. I tell you though, as a former builder myself, this is no coincidence.

Companies begin their business with little knowledge of who is who in their field. As a homebuilder, you deal with a wealth of different companies to bring a home into fruition. Most have a good pitch, but reality strikes when the house is underway and problems surface as they always do. As a builder (or anyone who uses subcontractors) gains experience, they also learn first-hand who the real professionals are and who has the "magic." They also learn from the mistakes and successes of others. So don't be surprised to find that when you obtain an account that incorporates success, honesty, credibility, and the magic that other accounts just like it will follow. You will also discover that you will eventually be a part of an elite group of professionals just like yourself. The "magic" will be a strong but unspoken force in which you all will be a part.

It is a fact that fusion marketing is an effective and powerful form of marketing. In the pressure cleaning industry, the fuse is long, especially with the growth of the Internet and social networking opportunities.

ARE TRADE SHOWS WORTH THE MONEY?

Hardly anything will communicate your intentions to prospects like a trade show. There is something about talking to prospects eye-to-eye and belly-to-belly to communicate unspoken words. This tactic is the real deal!

Your prospect will sense your passion for your service or product whether you are selling pressure cleaning or computer widgets. The bottom line in selling is a transference of feelings. If I can make you *feel* about my product or service the way I feel about my product or service, you are going to break your neck to purchase my product. If I have a sincere desire to fill a customer's need and know my product or service is going to scratch where he itches, I not only have a sale, but probably a residual buyer and friend.

"Nobody really cares how much you know until they know how much you care." It is not wise to think a trade show is going to get you money rolling in right away. More than anything, it will establish goodwill between you and those that attend. A trade show is a good vehicle to use to get to know your prospects. Let them know who you are. They should see that you care about their property. You care about their environment. You care about their individual concerns and they are not just another job to you. If you project the appropriate impression, they will use your product or services when needed. Don't expect the phones to ring off the hook from trade shows. Do expect to spend many hours one-on-one educating prospects and listening to stories about everything. But that's OK. Remember, your business is much more than the basic service you provide. Sometimes people just need to be heard. Listen and embrace the moment that you are able to enrich someone's life just by being a sounding board.

Don't get involved in trade shows if you are not willing to play psychologist now and then. Most of all, just be willing to listen.

Speaking of psychology, let me give you a typical scene that happens so often at home and garden shows. You have a beautiful booth set up with signs that communicate exactly what you do. You have gone to great efforts to have plenty of "hands on" props. Pieces of decking boards and cedar shakes that are many years old restored and preserved and are displayed for visual effect attention grabbers. You have many breathtaking before and after pictures of homes that you have cleaned. You are the authority. You are educating homeowners left and right. You are feeling great and are beyond proud of your knowledge and your business.

In a rush, a young lady scuttles into your booth, her

husband swiftly behind her. "Look honey. This is what our house needs so bad!" She points out a pair of pictures of a home that was cleaned. Her husband, of course, has his arms folded, a toothpick in his mouth, which he removes long enough to utter some words about how this is some kind of rip off and that he could do a better job than that anyway.

What to do? What to do? First, pretend you didn't hear the comment. Take a deep breath, walk over to the couple, and as he replaces his toothpick, ask them (looking only at him) if you can be of help. Chances are the wife is going to be full of questions. The awkward position here is that the husband thinks he is an authority on pressure cleaning. Why, he used a pressure washer one time back in the '70s to get

Make sure your setup is open and inviting to your prospects. Your display should be placed in a manner so that everyone can easily see your props and pictures. Always smile and greet people as they stop by.

mud off a truck his dad rented. The challenge here is to make this man look good in front of his wife. We men are weird creatures. You don't have to believe this method, but sadly enough it works.

So, as we begin our sometimes challenging endeavor to make the husband appear intelligent to his wife, we must listen carefully. Remember, this guy wants to be the macho man in front of his wife. The wife will often ask you how you made the house so clean that it almost appears that it was painted. The husband interrupts before you can answer. "All they do is spray bleach on the house and rinse it off. Anybody can do that."

As I said, you must dig deep to locate a minute morsel of truth or intelligence and with a little work, there it is! You look back at the man, and with surprise you state something like, "That's amazing! Our products, while environmentally friendly, contain the active ingredients that are in bleach." Smiling, you look at him and his wife and say something like, "How did you know that?" This is the time where his arms usually unfold. If appropriate, you tell his wife he must be one of those guys that can just fix everything around the house. Then immediately back to the husband. "So, you have done some pressure cleaning before?"

Now the guy is actually friendly because he's not threatened. As he tells you of his experience with the muddy dump truck, you search deeply for any truth in which you can again build him up in front of his wife. Then move the conversation in to what he does for a living. When he tells you, be respectful and convey that in his line of work he must be much too busy to be bothered with cleaning the exterior of the house. SOLD! I don't care if he is a doctor or a ditch digger, it will be hard to pass that assumption up in front of his wife.

The key factor here is to remain truthful. Sometimes finding the truth in a situation like this is more than challenging. Be patient. Do not be defensive and be polite. Sometimes it is hard to hold your tongue when everyone tends to come across with an attitude that they know more than you.

Remember how much technology has been introduced to our industry over the last several years. Unless you are involved, you would not know. It would be easy to put these "know it alls" in their place, but then no one would win. You'd lose a potential future client and our industry as a whole has been scarred.

Be prepared for these situations at trade shows. You set the standard. Be professional and keep an open and welcoming booth. Speak professionally and dress up for the occasion. Smile at your prospects, shake their hands, look at them in the eye and eat lots of breath mints. Again remember, no one will care how much you know until they know how much you care.

Make sure your setup is open and inviting to your prospects. Your display should be placed in a manner so that everyone can easily see your props and pictures. Always smile and greet people as they stop by.

Chapter 7

Laying the Foundation to Build Your Marketing

L et us begin with the core problem of marketing in general – most of all, pressure cleaning marketing and service quality. What must you improve? How do you learn? How about some techniques that really work?

First, you must understand what people are really buying. What are you really selling? Do you know where in the market your business is positioned? Do you know your prospects and their buying behaviors? Most of all, what are you communicating to your clients and prospects?

If I sell a car, you can see, touch, feel and experience that new-car smell. Pressure cleaning, by contrast, is invisible until after it is sold or performed. In fact, pressure cleaning is no more than an idea or thought and does not even exist when you buy it. If you go to get a haircut, you can't see, feel or try it out before you buy it. You order it, then you get it. Likewise, you just can't sense much about a pressure

98

cleaning – or any other service for that matter. You can't try on a dentist like a new sports coat. You can't smell a good architect, painter or shoe repairman. (You might be able to smell a bad one!)

In fact, in most cases, you buy your services sight unseen. What's worse is they usually don't have a price tag. You have to call two or three and hope you get a winner. To counter the price-tag problem, I sincerely urge all companies to consider setting up packages. Then be firm.

A large advantage of having set packages is that if a customer calls today for a price, you can give it to them over the phone. Another advantage is that if they decide to have the work done and call you back in six months, you will give them the same price. I experienced many embarrassing moments when I was young, giving different prices to a customer or trying to explain to some client why their house cost $100 more than their neighbor's house I did the month before. Set pricing and set packaging enables you to be consistent.

HOW TO SET UP PACKAGES FOR PRESSURE CLEANING

To eliminate miscommunication, we have packages for builders and general contractors as well as for other divisions of our company. Before these packages were everyday parts of our business, we often were challenged by customers pleading, "I thought this was included in that price." When you perform the same services for customers over and over,

> ## "The Shortest Way to do Many Things Is to Do One Thing at a Time."
>
> – Samuel Smiles (1812-1904)
> Physician & Writer

it is very wise to create a menu of services. Like McDonald's, a combo one is a combo one; it is their responsibility to know what a combo one is. This marketing strategy is not only an excellent marketing tool, it is also a tremendous time saver, and is convenient to offer add-on services.

Once your packages are established, it is not necessary to repeat every item on the checklist back to the customer when they place an order. A simple confirmation of "dress up package" is all that is necessary. The wonderful thing about packages or a menu of services is that you can modify them for literally any pressure cleaning application.

Notice, at a full-service car wash, they will have a basic wash for $10.95. Then other packages following that often reach up to $175 or more. Of course, each package up to the top offers a little more than the previous package.

Here is an example of the different packages we offer to our new construction contractors and homebuilders. The menu of services you see here is included in our information packet titled New Construction/Residential Division Menu of Services. Keep in mind that these packets are intended for marketing. The nuts and bolts of how to perform these packages are in our training manual and are much more explanatory without all the descriptive sales language.

New Construction/ Residential Division Menu of Services

The Foundation Package

A Foundation Package is a thorough cleaning of the masonry foundation and steps. A certified technician scrapes excess mortar from brick, then applies the proper solutions to clean brick or other substrate to its pristine condition.

Cleaning detergents and pressure vary upon the type, texture, color, composition and surface of the brick or other substrate. Exterior walls are gently rinsed at this time to assist and assure painters of a clean bondable surface.

The decks, patios, porches, stoops, sidewalks and entranceways are all rinsed for a cleaner, safer workplace and a professional, inviting street appeal for potential buyers!

Foundation Package $175.00 (Standard Size)

Note that these are just sample prices and don't necesarily reflect our current rates.

Dress-Up Package

Our clients who receive our Dress-Up Package are among the most quality-oriented and successful builders in the state. The objective of this package is to prepare the home for its formal presentation to the buyers. We do this by cleaning, "spitshining" and polishing every portion of the project we can see. Our job is to make the builder look good!

For residential contractors, this is ideal just before walk-thrus or showings. The Dress-Up includes a house wash-down, removal of construction dirt from soffits, siding, brick, windows, porches and decks. A Dress Up, in most cases, is the final touch before the homeowners take possession of their new home. It will leave the home in showcase condition!

It will reveal the detail incorporated in the woodwork, the unique definition displayed in the masonry, the smooth and intricate skillfulness of the painter and will pull all of these features together to have this home display its elegance and superiority.

A walk-thru is stressful for both the builder and buyers. The buyers are preparing to sign a 30-year commitment, spending more money than they ever will again in their lifetime. Their stress level is on 10! A builder sacrifices months of his life, hard work and sweat and has an emotional connection with the home, which becomes an extension of his pride and abilities as a professional. The buyers walk the house with the sole purpose of criticizing, nitpicking and locating every flaw imaginable. The builder's stress level is on

10! A spot of mud at the entrance in reality is a spot of mud; however, this could be all it takes to send buyers over the deep end, getting their defenses up and the start of a long and costly punch list.

A Dress Up in conjunction with a Concrete Package will provide breathtaking street appeal and is the finishing touch. Homeowners will park on a clean street and walk on an immaculately clean driveway and spotless sidewalk. Their defenses are down, and the anticipation of entering the home is a positive experience. They can see and feel that the builder has in fact taken care of all the details.

Dress Up Package $175.00

Concrete Package

This package includes a detail clean of all flatwork to include driveways, sidewalks, porches, stoops, patios, pool areas and more. HydroTech's light-duty concrete cleaner is applied and scrubbed on the surface, then pressure cleaned to a detail finish with a 15-degree nozzle and/or a surface cleaner for concrete. Other chemicals are used as well, depending on the composition and molecular structure of the stains. When requested, we also flag the flatwork with caution tape to prevent vehicles or walking traffic from soiling your finished product. The results are incredible! Your home will be the showplace of the neighborhood!

Concrete Package $ .12/sq. ft.

Garage Detail

This includes a detail cleaning of the garage floor as well as spraying off the garage walls. A wealth of construction stains such as paint, joint compound, glue, mortar, caulk and mud is removed with this service. Just as with the Concrete Package, we use a light-duty concrete cleaner and/or other chemicals depending upon the molecular structure of the stains. There is an extra charge for extreme cases of paint removal from the garage floor.

2-Car Garage	$50.00
3-Car Garage	$75.00
4-Car Garage	$100.00

The Paint Prep Package

For new construction on painted wood surfaces, this package is basically a Dress Up. The exception is that soap and an etching compound are used to help remove construction debris and mud. A complete wash-down of the house using a little higher pressure assists the painters by allowing them to apply paint to a clean surface. This allows the paint to adhere better to the surface so the paint will last longer.

Paint Prep Package	$.15/sq. ft.
	$125.00 minimum

THE BENEFITS OF PACKAGING

The benefits of offering set packages to your customers are way too many to list; however, a few are definitely worth mentioning. First, packages set you apart from the fly-by-nighters. They show potential clients that you know what you are doing and have a system in which you operate your business. It also eliminates miscommunication. That is a perk that everyone will enjoy. It alerts the client to their responsibilities. (You cannot very well clean a garage floor that is full of lumber.)

Packages offer clients choices. If the price is over budget, they can eliminate a package as opposed to the whole job. Packages also maintain a scope of work so you don't end up performing a ton of miscellaneous cleaning at no charge.

Once a package is complete, it has a definite parameter and is easy to identify as complete.

LEVELS OF CLEAN

Just as packaging opens many doors in your marketing efforts, so does offering different levels of clean. For years, our company was bombarded by objections that we were just outrageously expensive. We were always able to justify our price and usually get the job with a good bit of explanation and sometimes a good bit of invested time with new clients.

That explanation, of course, would begin with a question to the client. Just what degree of clean would you like to achieve? We have quoted to you our "extreme clean," which can actually be considered a restoration. This scenario would usually take place when estimating sidewalks or garages for shopping centers or high profile office centers where image is important. This questions would usually get us the job by alerting the prospect that they were probably not comparing apples to apples. A consultant friend of mine, David Frink, suggested I use a selection sheet labeled "The Five Kinds of Clean." This sheet has almost completely eliminated price shoppers and the need to explain to every new client our standard pricing. Now, they generally just ask for a different level of clean IF we are over their budget. If the customer wants it, we can deliver it.

Now we don't lose the job just because the customer cannot afford our superior services. These options also make it easy for the customer to have their shopping centers cleaned several times a year. Check out the following menu that has made it possible to fit almost any company's budget!

Five Kinds of Clean

Level One: Power Flush
- High volume water flush of all surfaces including curbs, walks and corners.
- Your option for litter, dust and dirt, including the nooks and crannies.

Level Two: Soap and Rinse
(All Level One Services, PLUS)
- Pre-treat entire surface areas with soapy solution.
- High pressure rinse of all surfaces.

- Your option for litter, dust and dirt, drink spills and other light stains.

Level Three: High Pressure Spot Cleaning

(All Level One & Two Services, PLUS)

- Pre-treat oil spots with grease softening agents and detergent solutions.
- Pressure clean oil spots with 200 degree HOT WATER and over 4000 lbs. of pressure
- Your options for litter, dust and dirt, drink spills and heavier spot cleaning.

Level Four: Comprehensive High Pressure Cleaning

(All Level One, Two & Three Services, PLUS)

- Pre-Treat and pressure clean using enclosed surface cleaning devices to cover all areas of concrete to be serviced.
- Rinse walls and columns up to four-feet in height.
- Your option for litter, dust and dirt, drink spills, oil spots and surface cleaning.

Level Five: Restoration

(All Level One, Two, Three & Four Services, PLUS)

- Pre-treat and remove gum
- Pre-treat and remove rust and other stains using stain specific solutions.
- Your option for Complete Restoration and Renewal.

This is the answer for so many companies that know only one way to approach a project. I know because I struggled for years trying to yell that we were THE BEST! The fact is that some companies just cannot afford the best. They often want to do business with you, but just cannot afford top-drawer quality. This menu is a great way to keep the businesses that cannot afford the best we have to offer.

After awhile of courting, they may just be able to afford a REAL clean that will allow you to show your stuff. When you show it, make sure it is worth seeing and not open for debate.

When a product goes south, that's easy to see. My watch stopped working. The new brakes did not brake. Is this milk supposed to be lumpy? Knowing when a pressure-cleaning job is bad is much more difficult, as is the case with any service. Make certain when you do get the opportunity to show your stuff, you knock their socks off. This will eliminate questions that may arise, just as with any services. Was that good advice from our real estate agent? Was that really a good carpet shampoo in our home? Was my car really repaired correctly? "Look Doc, I still have back pain and you want a check anyway?"

Settling a dispute with a service can be long and costly. You face prospects literally shaking in their boots waiting for the shaft. They are looking for any mistake you can possibly make. They are scared of the unknown and of course the known contractors they have dealt with in the past. This is where your marketing must start, with the understanding of their fears.

This information reflects how a growing number of

successful companies are following important marketing and life principles from planning presentations to publicity. These futuristic entrepreneurs focus more on relationships and less on the old features and benefits. They focus on reality and on achieving "better" reality, while recognizing the powerful influence of perception. They are learning more seemingly irrational ways in which people think and act. They recognize the tremendous impact of tiny things, they understand the near impossibility of being heard, much less understood. Our busy and over communicated society is one of complexity. Perhaps one of the oldest and proven truths of marketing history is that of simplicity. I will say that again. Perhaps one of the oldest and proven truths of marketing history is that of simplicity. It may not be easy, but it is simple to do the right thing.

These ideas, herein, may seem new, fresh and even unusually original. Truth is, they are old, proven and guaranteed to work. However, when you start thinking through these ideas more broadly and deeply and begin applying them to your business and products, you will find dozens of better ways to grow your own business. The magic is not a secret! Doesn't anyone get it? Good service sells!

"You Can't Build a Reputation on What You Are Going to Do."

— Henry Ford

Fix Your Service

Service quality has sunk to such an all-time low that if no one complains, it's considered a good thing. The "tip" has become more of a reflection on the customer than the service that is received. Meanwhile, you wait 40 minutes for your steak, you eat it cold and choke it down with the melted ice from your iced tea, which was consumed 30 minutes prior to your meal. You literally send fireworks up to gain the waiter's attention for your check, which, when you receive it, there is a charge for the shrimp cocktail he forgot to bring. Helloooo. Is anybody home? Is it just me?

What about the $180 a night, five-star hotel?

True story. I fly into Atlanta and attempt to check in. The clerk is clean and neat, but not exactly a rocket scientist. (I think his name was Darrell.) It is about 10 p.m., and I still have to set up the conference room and put my personal items away, which should take about two hours. I was in a little crunch for time, to say the least. A good night's rest is in order to be alert for our 7:30 seminar the next morning. Twenty minutes pass by as Darrell attempts to run another customer's credit card through. By now, I am fidgeting, checking my watch and really getting anxious about the seminar.

Finally, Darrell announces, "Next please." I look behind me to assure that it is indeed my turn. No one was there, so with my limited education I concluded I must be "next please." I step forward and happily give my name, reservation number and credit card number that had secured my room, as well as the conference room for the next three days. Darrell politely does his thing on the computer, and calmly tells me I have no reservation and the conference room is scheduled for some IBM function for the rest of the week. He worked sporadically trying to locate my reservations while I am a bundle of nerves creating visions of would-be seminar attendees burning me at the stake. He finally calls for help from "someone in the back." Well, "someone in the back" turns out be his brother Darrell. He spoke before thinking, as his words were not chosen very well. "Yep," said someone in the back, "looks like it. Bummer. Yeah, and we are completely booked. Can they take him across town?"

In a near rage, I am holding every fiber in my being from reaching over the counter and... "What's the problem?" snapped a deep militant, authoritative-type voice from the distant corridor. Darrell and his brother Darrell explain the situation to G.I. Joe, who obviously needed to be a drill instructor in the military or a poster child for the TV show cops. He then asks me for my reservation number, as if I were a speeder finally caught by a highway patrolman.

"Credit card and driver's license," he demanded. I handed them over, feeling like I had committed a crime and the only way to prove my innocence was for G.I. Joe to find something with my name, registration, birth certificate and/or blood type listed. "There it is," said the drill sergeant, completely oblivious to my presence. He began explaining how Sarah "screwed everything up," to Darrell. "This is so funny. Sarah must

Credit card and driver's license

have double booked the east wing."

This incident alone concluded about 11:45 p.m. Seminar attendees had similar experiences. One wife called and the clerk had misspelled the last name, so the wife was told he never checked in. The toilet clogged in my room so they moved me to another. My wife called and they told her I checked out an hour after I checked in. We were double billed for the rooms.

WE made the seminar happen despite the confusion and hysteria. You can bet I will NEVER hold another seminar there. This is how we learn. Let's learn with other people's money. No matter how many full color, glossy, ritzy ads I see about this hotel, the memory of my experience cannot be removed.

WHY HAS SERVICE GOTTEN SO BAD?

Situations similar to these happen all the time. I believe it is because companies cannot prove with hard numbers that investing more in customer service, improving or creating customer service systems and increasing salaries will create more profits. Most companies squeeze the absolute maximum out of a dollar and their people until somebody screams – usually the customer.

Personally, I believe you should pay your people so much money that they cannot afford to leave. Then expect the best from them. Make it clear that the customer is the reason we are able to live and prosper so well above industry standards.

How to Create a Better Reality

If you are like me, sometimes you may be so proud of the company you work with that occasionally you forget to take off your rose-colored glasses. For you young whipper snappers, "rose-colored glasses" is a term used for people that may live in a world that's just a little too optimistic, too positive, therefore "rosy." There is nothing wrong with pride and confidence in its place. However, let's take a closer look at your business. Let's call this a "reality check."

List the top four reasons you think your clients buy from you:

1.
2.
3.
4.

Determine your best customers from sales records:

1.
2.
3.
4.
5.
6.
7.
8.
9.
10.

Take your top four clients to lunch and ask them why they buy from you.

Find out what they like *most* about your company.

Find out what they like *least* about your company.

Compare your list and the clients' REAL reasons for buying from you. This is eye opening.

Now try this exercise:

List the top four reasons you think desired potential customers do not buy from you.

1.

2.

3.

4.

Take each of these potential clients to lunch and ask them why they don't buy from you.

1.

2.

3.

4.

Compare your list and your desired potential customers' list. (*Caution:* Companies have been known to gain a few clients by using this method.)

This is not an exercise just to read. This is an exercise to *do*. I assure you that just reading this will not increase your profits one cent. You must do this and expect rewards! Take action and control over your destiny. The money is there. All you have to do is disperse the right energy to make it yours.

If you performed this exercise in the precise manner I

described for you, it will work because now you have the vital information to create for yourself a "better reality." You now have an important list of goals to vastly improve the marketing of your business and what your business is communicating.

The actions you have taken with this exercise by showing your clients and potential clients that you really care is marketing that money cannot buy. You have taken a personal interest in their concerns as opposed to just trying to get in their wallet. Businesses will be caught off guard and will be refreshed to see some old-fashioned customer service first hand!

Knowledge in itself is not enough. It takes action, perseverance and determination. You can have all the information of a genius in your field; however, without action, it is all washed. Making a cake may be your goal. Knowing the recipe is important. Having the ingredients is easy. Putting them together to make the cake is the action that reaps the rewards.

THE BEST PRODUCT AND SERVICE

I recall when I first began in business. I had sold myself on the idea that if I were able to deliver the best product and service available, then my success would be inevitable. I spent thousands on research and development knowing that if I did not have a solid product and service, I had nothing.

The industry was so small it seemed as if we were definitely setting standards for our industry. The cost of keeping on top and delivering the best product and service to our ability became standard, but also expensive. We were missing balance.

I then decided that with all the cost of developing systems and processes, I actually needed more sales to support the unsurpassed product and service we were delivering. It was costing us a great deal.

I turned my focus on sales and marketing. If we were to sell more and bring in more revenue, that would take care of the research and development problem. Marketing was easy because I was confident in our company's abilities and reputation. Our sales soared. But we still lacked balance.

As a result of tremendous growth, we hired people from various walks of life to service the massive amount of business we had generated. I learned quickly just because a person interviews well doesn't make them a team player with the same values that you hold dear to your company. Different personalities, values, attitudes and images swarmed around our business with our logo pasted on their vehicles and uniforms. Knowing that the image of a business was vital to success, I focused my energies on the image we were setting within the company. Then I focused on the image we were generating to the public.

No one buys anything from a company they do not trust. Without the proper image, failure is certain.

I then turned my energy toward our people. Certainly if everyone prospered, was properly motivated, paid well above average, given responsibility and rewarded well with bonuses, and given a full benefits package their self esteem would be raised, their work would meet our high standards, and we would all succeed together! Sounds like an idea, but we were still missing balance.

I learned the hard way that not any one department of a business will deliver you success. I heard it illustrated one day that it takes balance of ALL the departments to assure success. However, there is one vital element that we did not mention. Without it, we are assured financial failure: PROFIT.

Without profits, we are just chasing our tails and wasting energy. The illustration I heard on this topic created a vivid reality in my mind of the importance of profit. Imagine, if you will, a juggler that is juggling five balls, working steadily at keeping all five balls in the air. This is similar to running a successful company. Four of the balls being juggled are white. One is labeled product or service, another sales and marketing, another image, and another is labeled people. In addition to the four white balls there is one red one. On

> "To become successful you must be a person of action. Merely to 'know' is not sufficient. It is necessary to know and do.
> – Napoleon Hill

this ball is the word profit. At all times, the juggler must remember that no matter what happens, DON'T DROP THE RED BALL!

Everything we mentioned earlier is vital to the company's success. The big things, the small things, and especially a balance of all things. If you cease to make a profit you will survive only a short time. If your air supply is cut off, you may live for awhile, but the bottom line is that soon you are going to die. So it is with making a profit. Without it you are just counting the seconds 'til the end.

I am reminded of the Star Wars sequel, "The Empire Strikes Back." Yoda, the Jedi teacher, tries to implant into Luke Skywalker the means of engaging the "force" that is the greatest power in the universe. Luke whines to his teacher, "I am trying! I am trying!" Yoda says to his pupil, "Luke, there is not try. There is either do or not do." I encourage you to "do." Be someone who makes things happen. How? In the words of a famous shoe manufacturer, "Just DO it!"

LESSONS IN LIFE

I learned as a very young businessman that I could gain a whole lot from the experiences of people around me, lessons that I could store in my tiny library of wisdom. I went to school in the late 1970s, a time when my life could go either way… a walk on the wild side, or a definite commitment to ethical righteousness.

I met a man named John Davis. We took an instant liking to one another, to the point that after knowing him a few months, I wanted to be just like him: honest, outgoing, compassionate, and most of all, "cool."

But that's not the biggest gift John gave me. He taught me how to trust people, how to give of myself and most of all, he modeled an unconditional friendship. I didn't always have to be "cool" or "perfect." He was always there. Little did I know, but by hanging around him, I was becoming like him.

All of us tend to model ourselves after those who are close to us, even if we are not aware that we are doing so. Modeling is how we learn in life, and how we develop our personalities. As a result, anyone who has known me for very long knows that I am a firm believer in keeping good company because you can't hang around with skunks and not expect to stink.

Role models can teach us how they overcame adversity and tell us the things they did and didn't in their drive to become successful. One of the many things I learned from John was that ordinary people can accomplish extraordinary things if they practice extraordinary discipline – if they refuse to be denied the pursuit of their dreams. Let's face it, if we are not getting better, we are getting worse. So I constantly look for new role models to study who might teach me new lessons. That is the key word: study! You cannot be afraid to adopt someone else's ideas and make them your own. But don't just copy good ideas, develop and build upon them.

When I hear someone say something I like or am interested in, I borrow it and make it mine. The key is to always learn from others. Learn from their mistakes, successes and failures, but always learn! People have things to teach us if we are receptive and have an open mind!

Chapter 8

What is Your Position in the Market?

"Your Actions Are So Loud, I Cannot Hear a Word You Are Saying."

PERCEIVED VALUE

Successful marketing must start with your position in the market. Marketing position, in layman's terms, can best be described as a company's perceived value and reputation to the public. It is what the community believes about your business, not your mission statement. It is not what you think you convey to the public, but what the public actually believes about your business.

Market positioning is much like politics, or a political campaign. You must take a stand on issues involving your industry; thus, being solid and standing firm on certain issues. A company may advertise technology, research and innovation; however, its position in the market may be "the local business with a track record for rudeness."

A good example of marketing position is that of

my personal veterinarians, whose technology may be unsurpassed. I am confident of their skills and services. They could possibly be the best veterinarians in the state; however, their primary marketing position is that they have compassion for all animals.

Dr. Jones and his wife, Dr. Alphin, are active in no advertising other than the phone book and a few brochures. What is remarkable is after only four years, they are thriving with business every day. The answer is simple. They take a stand on several issues on the humane treatment of animals. They actively participate in the banning of greyhound dog races. Dr Jones told me that "over 100,000 greyhounds are put to sleep every year." Once their use to man is over, they are discarded like a worn-out piece of trash.

Dr. Jones and Dr. Alphin take applications from good people to adopt these precious animals and provide them homes. Dr. Jones said many of these animals require quite a bit of treatment to get them back to health. Every surviving greyhound they rescue receives complete, up-to-date treatment. They receive all shots, are spayed or neutered, micro-chipped and receive good dental care as well. They are also part of the founding members who put together an association to develop the Ashley Fund, which provides financial assistance for animal treatment that is needed when the owners may not be able to afford care.

It is possible to communicate this type of message and only have it destroyed by careless employees. Knowing all the facts about our doctor's practice would not mean a thing if a rude receptionist greeted me. I don't care if it is the high school kid they hire to bathe animals or the doctor that treats them. If they come across as gruff or uncaring, I will discount their previous position in the market as a fluke. The same holds true with your pressure cleaning company. You can put forth magnificent efforts in fundraisers. You can sponsor and promote food drives for the hungry. You can even gain media exposure by helping the homeless. These efforts are all marketing homeruns. Unfortunately, all it takes to destroy all of this good will in a customer's mind is a careless or rude drive in your company vehicle. Perhaps the public believes they are seeing the real company values.

What about the technician who stops by the bar on the way home? Toasted and a possible drunk driver with your company logo as a moving advertisement. Is this your real position in the market? What about the technician who parks your company vehicle outside the adult bookstore? You think I am being a bit too paranoid, do you? Remember that marketing is a balance of everything. I do mean everything. When your business begins to become more notable, this is when you must make every decision with a dose of wisdom. With notoriety comes the risk of persecution and judgment.

Dr. Jones' and Dr. Alphin's awards and special recognitions are many and prestigious. Is this the secret to having a glowing market position? I don't think so. I think that the awards and recognitions are by-products of their position in the market. More than once have I taken an injured bird, bunny or stray cat hit be a motorist into their care. They have nursed them to health, and we have never been charged for any of the emergency resources. This business is a role model for learning about marketing position.

Their marketing position, after only four years, is loud and clear! Is yours? They are community servants who have compassion for all animals. They are not known as being spectators. They are active in their industry and community and take a solid stand on sensitive issues.

Do they burn some bridges and lose some business? Sure. A few poachers, greyhound racing fans and folks who could care less about animal abuse will not be their customers. However, people like me who consider our animals as part of our families will always be loyal customers. Obviously, I am not the only animal nut out there as I meet others just like me with their furry friends flocking to their doors after only four years.

HOW DO I GAIN A GOOD MARKET POSITION?

Your position in the market cannot be bought. It cannot be advertised. It cannot be persuaded. It must be earned. The more you say, the less people hear. Your position in the market is entirely based on how you are perceived. Therefore, your marketing position could very well be the most powerful marketing weapon you ever employ. In regards to perceived value and your position in the market, your future is strongly determined by your actions today.

Perception by the public takes a great deal of work on a company's behalf. Often perceptions are not reality. Therefore, as a business owner, you have to be on your toes to assure any misconceived ideas are halted before they are spread. Imagine a grouchy old man and his wife are on a long trip and they pull into a full-service gas station. The attendant cheerfully fills up the car with fuel and washes the windshield. The man in the car shouts at the attendant, "It's still dirty. Wash it again!" The young attendant complies and this time he cleans the windshield as Michael Angelo was to paint a picture. When he finishes washing the windshield, again he smiles and he hands the man his receipt. The man in the car snarls angrily, "It's still dirty. Don't you know how to clean a windshield?" Just then, the friendly owner of the gas station walks up and asks the driver if he could see his eyeglasses. The owner takes a tissue, politely wipes the driver's glasses, and hands them back to the driver. The man places them back on and BEHOLD, the windshield is clean!

Even though the company did its job perfectly, the customer perceived a different value. Fortunately, the station owner was wise enough to remedy this perception before it was taken as fact.

Often, we can get caught up in the heat of such an episode that the ultimate victory is proving yourself right. No one wins in a disagreement with a customer, even when you are unmistakably correct. It is difficult to bite your tongue because we are all human. Sometimes it seems as if some people really need to be put in their place. We can justify our emotions by the actions of these people. It is probably a fact that if we were to unload verbally on such an unworthy excuse for a human being, all who know this villain would rejoice and shout praises to you. In reality, you will feel good for a fraction of a second, then realize you have just burned a bridge. Depending on the influence of the horrid excuse for life, he or she may shed some influence on your company's perceived value to others. Though that value may be incorrect, you still have to deal with the consequences of that perception.

How do I build a perfect company?

In order to deliver a concept or idea, you must first have a clear and concise blueprint in your mind of what you want your company to deliver. Simply put, you must decide what you want. You are the absolute source to your business. If you are the business owner, every minute detail should be clear in your own mind. You should know exactly what perfection looks like so you will know what your target is. This process of crafting the perfect company in your mind is crucial to your success and position in your market. Once you have the "perfect" company visualized n your mind, write all the qualities, traits and characteristics down on paper.

Your list might resemble something like this:
- Honesty
- Education
- Integrity
- Professional Image
- Profitability
- Residual Clients
- Industry Leader
And so on… .

The more details you have, the more likely you will be to achieve your business goals.

Once you have a hard copy, list all of the qualities and characteristics that you envision as part of your perfect company. This is your picture or blueprint.

Now bring this picture down and oppose it to your existing business so you can see where all the bumps and cracks exist. If you are just starting a business, you now have a target to shoot for when making all of your business decisions.

Before setting your list in stone, take this little quiz. The results were taken from *Guerilla Marketing* by Jay Conrad Levinson, perhaps the nation's authority on marketing.

How Important is Price?

Rate the following in the order that you think is important when people buy, 1 being first, and 8 being last.

____ Image

____ Advertising

____ Customer Service

____ Product

____ Location

____ Price

____ Technology

____ Merchandising

Guess what? The survey is in its exact order, price being sixth on the importance scale of buyers! That's very low considering that cutting prices is the primary focus of so many entrepreneurs. In the prospect's mind, these facts are helpful when considering your market position. You will want your position to set you apart from your competitors; however, you must sacrifice

You cannot be all things to all people. You must focus clearly. Many fear the thought of positioning their product or service. Why all the fear? Because standing for one thing means you cannot expressly stand for other things.

Positioning and focus are vital to a company's success. No two products or services are the same. Ask a sales or service manager what sets them apart from their competition and you will probably get a disappointing response. Even the most boring products can communicate differences, which

> "Learning is the essential fuel for the leader, the source of high-octane energy that keeps up the momentum by continually sparking new understanding, new ideas, and new challenges. It is absolutely indispensable under today's conditions of rapid change and complexity. Very simply, those who do not learn do not survive as leaders."
>
> –Warren Bennis & Burn Nanus
> Leaders: Strategies for Taking Charge

are central to effective marketing. Not too many decades ago, flour, pickles, catsup and sugar – just to name a few products – came in huge tubs. They were then sold as commodities at the local corner stores. Then Heinz, Gold Medal and P&G came along and turned these indistinguishable goods into distinctive brands and made billions.

These name-brand products are almost identical chemically. If people perceive differences in these products, certainly they will see a difference in your product or service. If you cannot see the differences in your product or service, look harder.

Lastly, a solid marketing position will make all of your marketing efforts more effective by maintaining the same theme. Make sure that you and all of your employees can be effective marketers just in casual conversation. Employees can hurt you if they don't know what makes your company special. It is disappointing to ask a person what their company does and they give a generic, indifferent, really don't care answer: "We powerwash." No one wants to hire a company whose employees just don't care.

On the other hand, a clear, distinct message that conveys what makes your company special can get everyone excited. Everyone who works with the company will feel valuable just by being a part of the team. This focus and consistency will also get your marketing communications humming the same tune, and your messages displaying a common face. This makes it easier for the public to learn exactly who you are. Keep in mind that your market position is perceived value and reputation. It is as sacred as the name you earn for yourself in life.

A FINAL THOUGHT ON PERCEIVED VALUE

I am a true dog lover. At one point, I had four dogs and a cat and often dog-sat for my family or friends. In my opinion, a dog or dogs truly are man's best friend. No matter how bad I behave, they are still there with their tails wagging and sloppy kisses. I can leave home for one minute, realize I forgot my keys, and when I get back inside they all act as if I had been gone for a week and they are so excited to see me. They don't care how I look, how much weight I gain or even the stupid things I say. I can forget to let them outside or even bring them a doggie bag and they never have to forgive me because they never get mad at me. If I ever get too busy, one will always nudge me just the right time to let me know they desire my attention. To them, I am perceived as joy and love. I am special. I will offer the following prayer:

"Lord, please make me the kind of person my dog thinks I am."

– The Preacher's Illustration Service

Perceived value is vital in the big things and the small things.

Chapter 9

Are You a Pinto or a Cadillac?

"If you want a filet mignon, don't go to McDonald's."

If you needed heart surgery, would you consider three or four surgeons and then go with the lowest price? Of course you wouldn't consider such an absurdity; however, could it be true that we make decisions in other areas of our lives based on other subconscious checklists?

As business owners, we have the privilege of choosing our own image and reputation. We have the power to be known as a Pinto, a car with seats and an engine, or we can be known as a Cadillac, a car with plush interior, leather massaging seats, stereo, CD, TV, VCR and computerized luxury, i.e., elite first-class travel.

This is hardly a comparison, yet both are in the same industry– to provide transportation. The question you must ask yourselves as entrepreneurs is, "Am I a Pinto or a Cadillac?"

Inevitably, business owners inform me repeatedly that they are somewhere in the middle, and in my opinion, the danger zone. The middle or the "danger zone" is the epitome of mediocrity. It is not cold or hot and certainly not a profitable position at that. There are exceptions to this rule, and from lessons in history, you can see that they are in fact "those," exceptions.

Join me, if you will, on an adventurous reflection of how pricing has played a major role in determining product value and marketing success for many companies. Implement some of these ideas and your company may be in for an adventure, discovering extra profits you may already be earning!

THE PRICE IS NOT RIGHT!

In the early '80s, a new shoe appeared on the block. It was a good boat-type shoe and they priced themselves a good bit below the industry leader, "Topsiders." This new shoe competed toe-to-toe in quality, design and comfort, winning a foot in front in every area! The shoe, while an excellent product for the price, found itself stuck stagnant in the tracks of a lesser quality Topsiders competitor. Timberland changed one thing. They priced their shoes not only a little but well above their competitor. Sales boomed for Timberland, leaving Topsiders as the public's second choice. Both sales and profits skyrocketed, making them "the best."

In 1975, a kooky-looking guy came out with the first "gourmet" popcorn, a far stretch if you ask me. Four years later, the bow tie and Orville Redenbacher had the nation's number one selling popcorn in spite of the fact his price was two-and-one-half times higher than other leading brands!

131

How Can I get them to buy my service?

American Express made its mark and millions by charging more than its competitors and attempting for its name to be synonymous with wealth and prestige. Why? Because you liked it! I know you are thinking to yourself, "Why, I am a wise person who makes rational decisions based on objective analyses of costs and benefits." You be the judge.

Visa is accepted at nearly three times as many locations as American Express. You can pay back Visa right away or over time. You MUST pay American Express at the end of the month or be charged penalties and receive nasty notes. A Visa is usually free. You pay an annual fee for an American Express, even if you have perfect credit and a chunky savings account.

What do truly rational people want from their credit card? Utility relative to price, right? If you were being logical, you would want to use the card wherever you wanted to buy and the option to pay the entire amount to save interest or over time if you were in a crunch. A truly rational person would want to pay as little as possible for these benefits. A truly rational judge would carry a Visa. Why, then, do over 25 million Americans carry an American Express? It's because of prestige.

"Membership has its privileges." Let's get real here. Why do we wear a Ralph Lauren logo on our shirt as opposed to a K-Mart logo? Is a $300 Coach purse really better than the all-leather job at JC Penney? Rolex just can't keep time $4,000 better than the Seiko. Did you know that Honda makes Infinity? Black and Decker makes DeWalt. Toyota makes Lexus. These companies know from countless others in the past – the premium product or service is where the money is.

Charging more allows you the financial freedom to do the right thing when customers are not completely satisfied. It gives you the ability to provide unsurpassed customer service and truly exceed clients' expectations. The lesson here is that if we appeal only to our prospects' reason or rationale, we may have no appeal at all.

Focus on your position in the market, then set your price accordingly. Americans are more interested in austerity today than ever before. Why is it, then, that Neiman Marcus is thriving in sales? Bloomingdale's, while not the retail superpower it was in the '80s, is still hauling money to the bank by the truckloads? It is this thing called prestige. People buy what they want, as I have written and spoken about so many times before. People do not buy what the product is. They buy what the product DOES!

What feelings does obtaining your product or service create? Brainstorm and start writing down these feelings. Examples may include providing feelings of prestige, pride, glamour, peace of mind, security, safety, goodwill, intelligence, sexiness, honesty, cleanliness, power, beauty, wisdom. The list can go on.

Now, ask yourself, "What does my product or service really do?" If you sell a machine, does it provide security from downtime compared to an inferior product? Does a service you offer create pride because it makes your prospect

133

look good? Does it make them feel smart? Will it save them money in the long run, thus making them feel wise?

There are tons of possibilities. Write them down so you and your people are clear on what your product does. When you set your prices, don't always assume that the logical price is the smart price. Maybe the price you have is intended to make you look like a good value; make sure it is not making you look second rate.

DON'T PRICE YOURSELF TOO LOW!

Whatever you do, don't price yourself too low. Many years ago there was a company called Pathmark. They developed an all-purpose cleaner that was expected to take America by storm. This cleaner had all the elements of the perfect store brand. Its packaging plainly imitated the top seller in its category, Fantastik. Its chemical composition literally duplicated the top brand as well. The stuff was proven to work just as well as Fantastik, which sold for $1.79 a bottle. They called this product "Premium" and priced it at 89 cents a bottle! Permium was expected to put Fantastik out of business. Why not? Same amount, almost a dollar per bottle savings, does just as good a job. But to everyone's surprise, from 1980 until 1986 this stuff collected dust on grocery store shelves everywhere! Finally, the company decided they were misunderstood and people just didn't know the product. They went through all the bottles on the store shelves in America and placed stickers on each bottle.

The stickers read, "If you like Fantastik, try me." Still no one would try the product and they finally pulled the product off the shelves in early 1988.

Pathmark believed that even though their product was clinically outstanding, worked nose-to-nose as well as the competition, they had made one fatal mistake. The price was too low!

When your price is too low, the intrinsic value of you and your product can be discredited. Often, cheap can be too cheap. How do you get your price higher than the competition's? By offering a much higher perceived value. One sure way of gaining a higher-perceived value is just plain being a better value. Integrity is valuable. Honesty is valuable. Your word is valuable. It sometimes costs more to do the right thing. Make sure you charge enough to build and keep a good reputation.

In 1874, a man was born that would reinforce the ideas of perceived value. Tom Watson, the founder of IBM, believed that success in business required total involvement. He regarded his employees as extensions of his own family and ran IBM much like a family unit. He put high values on loyalty and mutual interest.

His first business on his own was as a piano and sewing machine salesman. He would transport his goods door to door by a horse-drawn wagon throughout the state of New York. He contributed his success to the manner in which he treated his customers.

As his small company called IBM evolved, he encouraged his salespeople to focus on the customer and service, and not on the product. He paid his people well and priced his products and services high enough to be recognized as a superior company that stood behind its sales. He worked hard to create a company image as one that was an important and responsible part of the community and world affairs.

His employees were taught that being good citizens was as important as being good businessmen.

Presidents Roosevelt and Eisenhower regarded Watson as an unofficial goodwill ambassador. Watson knew the importance of perception, even in his day. The same perception and qualities that made him a success as a piano and sewing machine salesman are the same perception and qualities that created one of the major business superpowers today.

PREMIUM PRICING

A final thought on premium pricing as a marketing tool. (Of course, if you know me, a final doesn't really mean finally. It just means we are getting there!)

I recall an incident concerning a small appliance store owned by an older gentleman named Joe, and located somewhere in Arizona. The store first belonged to his father and was eventually passed down. This store had survived for years and was now being fought head on by the huge electronic-appliance superstores, one of which had been built only two blocks away.

Joe and his father before him had always charged a premium price for their appliances. However, they had also earned a reputation of absolute honesty, quality and unsurpassed customer service. Repeat customers were not a problem. That was a done deal. It was the young newlyweds that were hitting every store in a ten-mile radius that were creating his challenge. They could come in the store, pen and paper in hand, asking detailed questions about prices, features, benefits and model numbers. When, after spending half an hour with such a couple and patiently answering all their questions, Joe knew he had done all their homework for them. They were now prepared with the ammunition they needed to visit the masses of discount stores. Joe then requested the order and received almost identical answers from every couple: "We want to look around at some other places."

How many of us have heard that line after completely educating a prospect? Let's take a look at how old Joe handled this opportunity.

Joe would tell the couples that he understood they were looking for the best deal possible because he did the same thing himself. He also told them he knew they were probably going to make a beeline to the discount store and compare the prices because he would do that too. Then he would lower his voice and give them a warm, genuine smile and proceed with his following little speech. "After you finish all your comparisons and you find this exact model at Discount Dan's for $350 less, I want you to think about one thing. You would get a great appliance at Discount Dan's. But when you buy the same appliance here, you get one thing you can't get at Dan's. You get me. I come with the deal. I stand behind what I sell. If it goes on the blink, WE come to you. I want

> ## "The price of greatness is responsibility."
>
> - Winston Churchill

you to be happy with what you buy. I've been here 30 years. I learned the business from my dad, and in a few years, I will give the business over to my daughter and son-in-law. So you know one thing for sure. When you buy an appliance from me, you get me with the deal. That means I will do everything I can to make sure you never regret doing business with me. That's a guarantee."

With that, Joe would wish them well, along with some humorous newlywed advice and a free half-gallon of ice cream for their interest. How far do you think young couples are going to get with Joe's speech ringing in their ears and a half-gallon of ice cream on their hands in Arizona when it is 100 degrees in the shade?

In a nutshell, it costs money to stand behind your product or service. It costs money to do the right thing. Insurance, taxes, social security. It costs REAL money to keep good people that take pride in themselves and your company. Pinto or Cadillac? The choice is yours.

An associate pointed out to me, "Steve, they stopped making the Pintos years ago." Point well taken. I wonder if others will get it.

Chapter 10

The Pricing Principle: How to Set Your Price

"Setting your price is similar to setting a screw. A good bit of resistance will make your business secure."

"There is just no way people will pay those prices where I'm from."

"How am I supposed to compete with the guy across town who runs ads stating that they will beat my price?"

"When I told them my price, they laughed at me because it was twice as high as they are paying now."

These are just a few of the concerns I hear at EVERY marketing seminar – especially the courses on pressure cleaning. The concerned parties are those who operate their businesses in an ethical manner, in a sometimes not-so-ethical industry. Taxes, worker's compensation, and general liability are just a few of the overhead costs of real businessmen and women. I do not even consider the person who purchases a cheap pressure washer, acid and bleach, and who does not pay his taxes to be competition. Neither should you.

History shows us that over the last 10 years, these guys will not even be in business an entire season. Most are scheming to make a quick buck, and when they find out it really is work and does take quite some skill and learning, they are off to another scam. That still takes so many lost jobs and income from those of us focused on professional pressure cleaning, money that was snatched from us by these fly-by-nighters. These are the individuals that can "beat any price." If you have no clue as to the effects of bleach on azaleas and don't care, you *can* beat any price. If you use the brute force of 4,000 psi to "clean" a deck and are not accountable for the damage, again you *can* beat any price!

So what is the answer to surviving in this industry while the fly-by-nighter is taking what could have been your business? That is just one of the questions we will answer in this chapter.

While discovering pricing as a powerful marketing tool, you will also see how to avoid some costly pricing mistakes. You can also create a good system for price setting in your business.

WE WILL BEAT ANY PRICE!

These could be the fatal last words of many companies. I have to admit, I used to get so mad when I saw these ads

I could spit nails. Now that's an ad campaign! JUST BEAT ANYONE'S PRICE. Just have no regard for taxes, insurance, proper solutions and accountability. Just do whatever it takes to beat any price. "Call around and get your cheapest price then call us and we will beat that." I think this is about the closest thing to pressure cleaning prostitution there is!

I have been so tempted to buy the same sized ad as these guys have. Right where their ad says "Guaranteed Cheapest Price," I'd like to run one that says "Guaranteed Highest Price." I would get the satisfaction of educating clients even if we didn't get one job.

As you can probably tell by my choice of words, I still get a little hot under the collar when on the subject of these get-rich-quick temps. I take special effort to NEVER advertise in ANY medium where one of these rocket scientists may have an ad. Do not do anything to allow the public to even consider these people as your competition.

In the meantime, what's the answer for going head-to-head with the cheapest priced company? Waiting it out? No, that won't work because there will be an entire new army of fly-by-nighters, beat-any-price knuckleheads next year, and the year after, and the year after.

Do you lower your price to be the cheapest? That is guaranteed to get you all the business you can handle. However, you cannot work for free without starving to death. Even if you could, it's only a matter of time before someone will beat your price. Price shaving doesn't take an Einstein. No one earns customer loyalty by having the cheapest price. Those customers are loyal to the price.

In reality, you must face the music and realize you cannot

compete with these types of businesses. If this business were your livelihood, why would you want to anyway? Set yourself so much apart that you could not even be remotely compared to these bad apples. The fact is that time will determine the survival of the fittest and you cannot survive competing with the part-timers that do not operate under the guidelines of the law. They cannot survive unethically because "stuff happens" and when it does, they will disappear just as they always have. Setting your prices should be a relatively simple task.

LESS IS NOT BETTER!

If no one complains about your prices, then your prices are way too low!

Keep in mind our industry has evolved from a backyard business hobby. Today, there are educated, skilled professionals who are experts in this new and complicated industry. Customers are accustomed to not paying much more than a "tip" for pressure cleaning services. Expect to be questioned. If everyone complains, your price may be too high.

So where is the best resistance when setting your prices? Setting your prices may take a little tweaking. Setting your prices is similar to setting a screw; a good bit of resistance will make your business secure. Most businesses NOT in our industry should have what I call a 25 percent "squeal factor." That simply means when one purchases a product or service, about 25 percent of the people are going to squeal about the high cost. This is a good thing. This is a great targeted resistance for most any business.

You figure about 15 percent are going to complain no matter what you charge. Then there are those who want to "deal," and of course the ones that are just plain scared and mistrustful and think no matter what price you give them, they are gonna get stuck. The other is the group who already had a price in their mind and budgeted what they believe to be a fair price.

THE PRESSURE CLEANING INDUSTRY IS NOT MOST ANY BUSINESS!

That is the purpose of this book. This business is unique and requires a different approach. If we followed these standard guidelines for most businesses, we would go broke. I believe the squeal factor in our businesses should be a solid 50 percent! In our personal pressure cleaning business, we have over a 75 percent YELL factor from new clients, but that's ok. We pride ourselves on a solid reputation of expertise and remaining accountable for our actions year after year. Once the yelling is over, then we have the customers for life!

By the way, customers don't yell when you make a mistake and are accountable for your actions. Thankfully, the yelling is only temporary during the customer's education of our services. Inevitably, when we do give a discount of a "deal," it tends to come back and bite us via an unsatisfiable customer, one who "claims" we tarnished a 20-year-old simulated brass light fixture, or one that just simply will not pay.

In this industry, the cheapest WILL NOT survive. The lowest price is literally guaranteed failure. Avoid the bottom. It is an inescapable pit!

THE DANGER ZONE

The middle is where the flocks of businesses want to rest. Most people believe that this is the safe zone. This is the "DANGER ZONE!"

Most entrepreneurs study the highs and the lows of their industry. Often by phone, others by research. Once the information is obtained, they try to decide where they fall on this quality spectrum. This unfortunate practice tells their customers exactly how good the company THINKS it is.

Is this how you set your pricing? If so, what are you telling your clients? Are you telling them you are really not that great, kinda middle-of-the-road, average or just plain mediocre? The middle price is a deadly position to be in because it communicates "We are NOT the best and neither are our prices, but both our services and prices are pretty good."

Contractors send out invitations to bid. Some get 50 or more responses. If you know that 35 percent of the bids are going to be within 10 percent, what is the magic that will make them pick you?

How to Get the Work

Premium pricing is the path to prosperity. Imagine, if you will, you have a company with top-of-the-line equipment. Your people are all uniformed, well groomed and well spoken. You have a position in the market as a trustworthy business that is a permanent part of the community. Your vehicles may not be new, but they are always clean and neat. Your drivers are friendly and courteous. Your business is part of the everyday lives of the city whether you have one truck or ten. You submit a proposal for $32,000 on a project. The low prices are in the mid-eight-thousands. The middle prices are in the 19- and 20-thousand-dollar areas. You get the job. How does this happen?

First of all, contrary to popular belief, very few businesses choose the lowest price.

Second, the proposal which you presented was without doubt professional – bound, full color, complete with job specifications, an introduction letter, references and an eager request for the job. The client is so curious as to why the large spread in your price, he asks to meet with you concerning your numbers. It is obvious he wants your company because of the message you speak to the community.

But how can you answer the most obvious question of all questions? How can you possibly be one-third higher than the second-highest price?

The answer is really quite simple. The process is a continued commitment to excellence. You have taken every measure to make your company the best company it can be. You have certification programs for each of your technicians. Your safety procedures exceed the standard OSHA regulations, and your insurance is well above their requested minimum.

You are involved in continued pressure cleaning education with the utmost of concern for your staff and all visitors on the job site. You operate by the guidelines set forth by the EPA, therefore protecting the interest of your client. You and your people not only know what chemicals to use and to neutralize, but you are also able to explain the process in detail to OSHA or EPA visitors. These procedures cost money.

When all is said and done and you have given your heart to the success of his project, you leave him with this: "Mr.. Client, we started our business some time ago. At that time we had to make a very important decision. We had to decide

Hands-on training at one of our pressure cleaning courses. If you want to charge premium pricing, you need to be properly educated.

then whether we were going to spend the rest of our lives apologizing for poor quality over and over, or were we just going to take the time to EXPLAIN price one time. We chose to explain the price. I am so glad we made that decision then and there, and Mr. Client, I know you are too."

> ## "Nothing great was ever achieved without enthusiasm."
>
> *– Ralph Waldo Emerson*

Every time I discuss this with a prospect, I feel more enthusiastic than the time I said it before. It also makes more sense each time I ponder the decision that I made.

PREMIUM PRICING WINS FOR EVERYONE

Premium pricing is the route to prosperity in this industry. However, you have to give 110 percent. Not just once, but day in and day out. The premium pricing needs to follow all of your residual work: shopping centers, fleets, vent hoods, restaurants, malls, new construction, residential, and the list goes on.

When you charge a premium price, people expect a premium service, and you *can* deliver a premium service. This is the scream that markets your company successfully. You can take care of your people that go the extra mile for you and the clients. Pay them dearly; you can take so much better care of your clients. Everybody wins! Get paid for your knowledge as well as your sweat!

(This is not an ad for our pressure cleaning course, of course. OK, it is.)

A woman was strolling the streets of Paris without a care in the world. She spotted Pablo Picasso sketching at a sidewalk cafe! Not so thrilled that she could not be slightly presumptuous, the woman asked Picasso if he would sketch her, and charge accordingly. Picasso obliged.

In just minutes, there she was with an original Picasso! "And what do I owe you?" she asked.

"Five thousand francs," he answered.

"But it only took five minutes!" she reminded him.

"No," Picasso said. "It took me all my life."

Again, charge for your knowledge, years and experience, not by the hour. I encourage you to excel in your business and prosper.

EXPERTS RELY ON PROFESSIONALS

Many years ago, I made my living as a general contractor building new homes. Now I have always pressure cleaned, but there was a time of about 12 years when I considered myself a part-time pressure cleaner and full-time builder.

As a young builder, I was always seeking new ways to cut costs. I would like to think that I have always been wise enough not to "skimp" on craftsmanship. I never really tried to haggle with my subcontractors on their prices because I knew that if a problem occurred in five years, I wanted them to stand behind their work. (Even if they would not, I would anyway.) But, believe me, I would make those lumber salesmen work hard for their money! Just as I did the lighting salespeople, the carpet and hardwood salespeople, all the way to the door, window and drywall salespeople. The way I saw it, a number two grade two-by-four is a number two grade two-by-four whether you buy it from Lowes, Eighty-Four Lumber or Home Depot.

Then I tried other ways of saving money. The first couple of houses I decided I would save about $8,000 per house by painting them myself. Man, $8,000 is a lot of money! I thought, "Hey, I was in the Air Force, and I painted just about anything that wasn't moving." So I took on the task of painting. This was going to be a piece of cake.

I began to paint the outside of the first house, and each time I would get started I would be paged, get a phone call or would have to meet an inspector or homeowner. I spent two months painting just the outside of that first house. That is after I had gotten all my friends, girlfriend and family to hold a brush for at least a couple of days. This small task turned into a monster of a job.

Then came the inside – the easy part – so I thought. I painted and painted. Every time I picked up a brush, I would get paged, called, or have to meet a prospective homeowner "right away."

I felt like my life consisted of nothing in the world but painting. I learned I hated painting. I was dreaming about painting. Oh my gosh. I was painting in my sleep. Paint was everywhere. I thought surely if I died and went the wrong way there would be a paintbrush with my name on it.

"Oh Lord," I pleaded, "If You just help me finish painting this house I will never ever try to paint another one again." I got trim paint on the walls, and, as if that wasn't bad enough, I would paint over that and then get some wall paint on the trim, then repaint the trim and get more on the walls and the floor.

A painter came by one day and offered to give me a price to finish. I was so happy I could have kissed him. I mean, how much could it possibly be? I was practically finished, except for touching up here and there. He gave me a price of $2,000. I thought the guy had lost his mind! Two thousand dollars? I told him it seems like he could have just about started the job from scratch for that. He then told me that it would actually have been easier to start from scratch than to try and repaint over what I had already done.

I did my best not to take it personal. I shook his hand and thanked him, but let him know there was no way I was going to pay two grand on a house that was just about complete. I did tell him to keep in touch because I knew I was not going to paint the house I was building next door for sure.

After about two more days of every spare moment I had with a brush in my hand this scraggly fella walked in with painter's clothes on. He smelled a little like beer.

"Need some help? I been paintin' about 20 some years." Against my better judgment, but out of desperation, I said,

"Sure. How much will you charge me to finish up?" He looked around for about 10 minutes, came back and said, "How 'bout 800 bucks?"

I said, "When can you start and how long will it take?" He told me he could start now, finish out the day and it would be done in two more days. I gave him my brush and began to sing his praises on my way out.

How ironic. Now I paint on canvas for pure enjoyment! And, although a recent accident has hindered my ability to do fine work, I look forward to bodily restoration someday, and I hope the good Lord will provide plenty of artist brushes, canvas and an easel up there for me.

Well, the next day the scruffy old guy started painting. I dropped by around noon and he was painting away. I couldn't really tell he had done much but it was getting done and that made my day. Before I left he asked if he could have half his money because he had been out of work awhile.

I didn't know him, but under the circumstances I agreed. I then left to attend to builder's business, as I should have been doing anyway, instead of playing painter. About two hours later, I saw the painter on the other side of town as he waved at me joyfully. I got back to the house under construction later that evening to find all my paint supplies, a $2,000 paint sprayer, and a $200 heater gone.

I called the number he gave me and got an irate woman who threatened to kill him if she ever saw him again. She assured me that I would never see him again. She was right.

I called the original painter that had stopped by with the $2,000 quote. That's what I paid him to finish my mess.

The pot of gold at the end of the rainbow is this

painter was a professional and we have had a fine business relationship for many years now.

I wish I could say that my lesson was completely learned there; however, I attempted on other houses, driveways, patios, and decks. I vowed to never attempt anyone else's trade after those couple of years. I think there's a word for someone who spends so much money making the same mistake again and again: STUPID!

DISTRIBUTORS FOCUS ON YOUR SUCCESS AND OFTEN PROVIDE YOU WITH LEADS

I told you that story to make a point about pressure cleaning industry distributors. At the close of every course, I get bombarded with phone calls and emails on how to make this cleaner or how to make that cleaner. How to make this machine, or how to make that machine. Remember the story of painting the house? Do what you know!

Several years ago, I started a nice workshop/storage building. My goal was to have it finished and decorated for Christmas, THAT Christmas. I was a general contractor, remember? I could certainly build my own storage building.

However, almost two years later it was still not finished. A friend ended up taking on the project so I could sell my house. That's what he does for a living. He builds decks, does remodeling and other types of construction. He told me that he and his guys would have had that building built from scratch in two days. It was a major pain in my anus posterior for TWO YEARS. I still had not learned. I will not do these kinds of things any more. Again, do what you know!

We have distributors in our industry who work their hind ends off for their customers. So what if you might be able to save a buck a gallon on this or that. What good is it if you save two grand on a pressure-cleaning unit if you don't have the support to keep it running when it shuts down!

When we have a pump go south, we take it to OUR distributor, Great Waves in Garner, North Carolina. When we have an engine down, 98 percent of the time it is back on the road within an hour. They stock parts just for us. If they don't have the part, they loan, not rent, for our company a machine until they get ours back on the road. If I need a mechanic on site right now, they will break their neck to get there. That's what they do.

Now, can I get a high-pressure hose somewhere else cheaper? You bet! But, there is the same word for that. Stupid.

How much money could I lose waiting on my units to be back on the road? They are focused on getting our business back in business. They are smart enough to know if I succeed, they succeed. They want all of their customers to prosper because we are in this industry together.

They don't just work on our machines either; they have been a great help in the computer area. Again, are they the cheapest price? No way Jose'. But I know it would COST me more without their focus and professionalism targeted on HydroTech's success.

Just like painting that house, you might be able to

make some chemicals, but what is the real cost? How many thousands of dollars do you lose trying to work on your own equipment? Or spend a day waiting to save $20 on a part? Your time is much more valuable. Making good contacts, writing proposals, working your PR list. Good distributors may be hard to find; however, when you do find one, they will save you thousands by allowing you to stay focused on your target!

Our training facility's policy and our beliefs are to put our contractors in touch with the most reputable and most respected distributors in their area. If they seem expensive, wait 'til the rubber meets the road and then decide if they are worth the price. The first time you KNOW you were deceived, find a new distributor.

For the contractors out there who have been toying with the idea of building their own units or equipment, consider this. Build a relationship with a distributor you can trust. Be 100 percent loyal to their company. They know that if you succeed, they are more likely to succeed. They really want you to be a star. Don't get ripped off, but pay a fair price or even a premium price. If we, as pressure cleaning contractors, would commit our focus on marketing our business and continuing education, we would surely prosper.

The distributor is vital in the success of the professional pressure cleaner. You find a distributor who values and wants to earn your business and you remain loyal. Don't be like the builder that tried to save some money painting when he should have been focused on making sales and customer service. I assure you, if you target your market and focus your energy on your business, you will gain far more wealth than looking at the grass that always seems greener on the other side.

Chapter 11

H ow to M ake a Sale

M any of you likely recall the first time you met your
husband or wife. Remember what was going through
your mind? Remember how excited you were? Do you
recall during the courtship phase of the relationship how
much attention you paid to detail? Am I underdressed or
overdressed? Does she like me in the black slacks or my
snug blue jeans? Does she like flowers or candy? Should
I open her door or will she think I'm a male chauvinist?
Should I be sensitive or a little macho? Do I play heavy
metal or the Bee Gees as we drive to our destination? I am
just not sure, so I will have boxes of CDs from Amy Grant
to ZZ Top, Bach to Mozart, and Garth Brooks to Willie and
Waylon.

Fellas, you have been there, and I know you can relate.
Ladies, I know you have been through your closets more than

a time or two trying on everything for just the right blouse, only to find out that it didn't match your purse. Let's not even discuss the formula for finding the right pair of shoes. I believe it has something to do with having every pair out of the box on the floor. Then there was the lipstick! Pink rose? Raspberry? Just how many shades of red are there? How about the perfume? Ok, I know you only had a few dozen scents, but does it say, "Come on big boy" or "I am pleasing to be around"?

Remember how important every little detail was to you? Can you recall even perhaps rehearsing lines that you wanted to say if you wanted to go steady, to the prom, or popping the big question for marriage? Sure you can! Guess what! If you're married, went to the prom, or even out on a date, you made the sale!

The above analogy is an excellent example of preparing for the sales call. Think of the homework you did in selling yourself to your spouse. Tell me, do you still brush your teeth and use mouthwash six times a day? Just a thought for the prospects and clients you now have. (Your spouse would probably still appreciate it too.)

The sales call, like a marriage, is just the beginning. The sales call to some can be a very intimidating experience. Yet if you think of where we have been thus far in the marketing series, you will conclude that the "Marketing Magic" – selling your product or service – is something you do for someone, not to someone.

Review the last few chapters and make sure you understand that selling is a transference of feelings. If I can make you feel good about my product or service, you will literally break your neck to obtain my goods.

Are you a man or woman of integrity? People of integrity are the ones that get ahead the fastest! Dr. Mortimor Fineburg, the author of *Corporate Bigamy*, interviewed 100 top executives. He asked the question, "What is necessary to go to the top and stay there?" Although they said many things, the common denominator that they all agreed on was to build honesty, character, integrity and, they threw in the word, "motivation." Many agreed that anyone who thought they could obtain success and remain successful without being honest was dumb!

Ability may bring you success, but it is character that will keep you there. A successful sales call begins with YOU personally. You cannot be one kind of person and another type of salesperson.

You may have heard the saying, "business is business." This has given the masses the right to exaggerate and even tell white lies in the name of business. The fact is you are who you are, whether you are out with the boys or alone with your child. There are no barriers.

There was another study by the Forum Corporation. This study involved 341 sales producers. They divided them into two categories: 173 were high producers, 168 were moderate producers. These salespeople were taken from many different industries: high tech, banking, insurance, petroleum, etc. The Forum Corporation found that all of the participants were basically even in their skills. Their techniques were the same. Their procedures, abilities, closing processes and presentations were all the same. What separated the top from the middle was trust.

Honesty is not only moral, it is practical. Are you trustworthy? Remember that you cannot be one kind of person and another type of salesperson.

WHAT IS THE MOST IMPORTANT PART OF THE SALES CALL?

The salesperson is the absolute most important part of any sales call. People don't buy based on what they hear. People don't buy based on what they see. People don't buy based on what you say. People buy based on what they hear, see and believe!

Do you recall perceived value? If you are not believable, you will not sell for long. I do know there are the con artists out there who will make a sale. However, we are talking about building a business career, not a one- or two-times sale

CREDIBILITY IS YOUR NICHE

You cannot make a good deal with a bad guy. If you are a good guy or gal, keep reading. If you are not, chances are this book will only serve as a temporary fix.

The sales call is an attitude with all the little things working for you. Do you have a good shine on your shoes? Do you have a smile on your face? Are your slacks pressed? Is your skirt or dress neat? Is your breath clean and fresh? Is your hair clean and in place? Are you overdressed or under dressed? Are you smoking or chewing gum? Are you neat and clean? Is your makeup fresh and properly applied? Are you on time? Are you professional and courteous? Are you respectful of your prospect's time? Do you leave in the allotted time or do you loiter and wear out your welcome?

These things are small, but they really mean the difference between making the sale and missing the sale, getting the proposal or missing the proposal, getting the spouse or losing the spouse. These are the details that will assure you success!

KNOW THY CLIENT

Knowing as much as you can about your client is as important as knowing about your product or service. The little things don't mean a lot, they mean everything! They are often the signs that a prospect reads to make their final decision. The signs, when read all together, generally read, "I care."

"We are continually faced by great opportunities brilliantly disguised as insoluble problems."

A few notes on what to learn about your prospects and clients. Do not limit the search just to business likes and dislikes. Before the sales call, find out what your prospects are like as human beings.

- What do they feel strongly about?
- What are they most proud of having achieved?
- What are some of the status symbols in their offices?

How do I do this if I have never met or even been in the prospect's office? That is exactly why you are where you are in life. Those who say I can't, won't. Those who try, succeed. (OK, but how?)

When you know your customers and some of their special interests and characteristics, you have a basis of really communicating with them. Knowing your prospect before the sales call means knowing what your customer wants. It might be your product or service or maybe it is something else. Maybe they are dying to talk about their new grandson. Maybe they are looking for recognition, respect, service, reliability, a friend or possibly many things we care about more than gallons per minute or restoring a deck.

A good book that contains "The 66 Question Customer Profile" is *Swim With the Sharks Without Being Eaten Alive* by Harvey Mackay. This book contains information on what you should try to learn about your prospects – from their political views to their favorite type of soda. It also tells you how to go about getting much of the information that you need.

When I visit a prospect's office, I am alert to everything around me. What can I find to relate to this individual on a personal level? Is it the huge sailfish mounted on his wall? Is it a picture of a large family on his desk? I inconspicuously take notes, especially if I am lucky enough for them to get busy on a phone call while I am there. My notes after a brief meeting, besides the obvious, would read something like this:

MEETING with JOE JOHNSON, DC. PROPERTIES,

- His wife's name is Peggy.
- His wife is presently coming down with the flu.
- Made sly remark about his boss.
- His son goes to State and is on the wrestling team.
- Hates former President Clinton, Hillary and Chelsea.
- Drinks caffeine-free Diet Coke, in the can.
- Has picture on the wall of himself and Johnny Cash.
- Has a picture of himself holding a huge fish.
- Secretary's name is Julie.
- She likes Rusty Wallace and Elvis Presley.

Once I have this information, I have enough knowledge and ammunition to make the next meeting memorable for my prospect. Every morsel of information I retrieve goes into my files. I am only human and can only remember so much. Yet, when I meet Joe again, possibly with a proposal, I will study his file thoroughly.

I will start off by asking how his wife Peggy is doing and if she ever got over the flu. If the situation should arise, I would ask if his son is still enjoying wrestling at State, or if he had any fishing trips lined up. I would be prepared to talk to him in his language. I would greet Julie by name and know something interesting about Nascar to possibly make her chuckle. I would take notes again just as I did on the first visit and collect information in each future meeting to build a relationship.

Enough investigating and common ground of interest is usually quick and fun. There is more to making the sale than exchanging money.

This is life. It is not a dress rehearsal. You gotta love it, live it and most of all grow from it, both financially and personally.

When you are in business for the long haul, you have to care. Your care in your career is not something that you can fake. It is for life. Believing in yourself and your product is an absolute necessity. In fact, if you are puzzled as to why a prospect would not want your product or service, then you are obviously sold on your business.

People who believe in their business have a much better closing rate than those who do not. Like I said, you can't fake it. When you honestly know that what you are providing for your client is going to help them solve a problem, you will succeed!

Given all the information above, it is clear that the first three steps to a successful sales call are:

1. Be a man or woman of integrity and trust. (Remember, it's not only moral, it's practical.)

2. Have an absolute genuine belief in your product or service.

3. Learn everything possible concerning your prospect.

Chapter 12

How To Handle Objections: Profiting From Personalities

Overcoming prospects' objections often causes many business owners to feel timid or out of place…kind of like a milk bucket under a bull: "I'm not sure I belong here."

The good news is that you do belong and some people, no matter how much you educate them, will attempt to put you on the defense. They feel it gives them a better position to "bargain." However, remain true to the strategies and themes that we are learning in this series and even in the would-be pressure situations, you will find yourself on the same side of your prospect continuing to earn their trust!

This section will cover the identity or personality style of your prospect. What kind of person he or she is and what ways will be best to communicate or persuade.

THE FOUR D-I-S-C TENDENCIES

Sociologists have discovered that of the many personalities people may have, there are actually only four categories that most all people tend to fill. The term for these characteristics is called "DISC TENDENCIES."

The four tendencies are as follows:

D – Dominance

I – Influencing

S – Steadiness

C – Competency

(I'll explain each of these in further details shortly.)

As a business owner, if you can identify which "tendency" is dominant in your prospect or client, you can adapt your communication style to reach him or her, and strengthen your sales calls and customer relations.

For example, have you ever asked someone a simple question that may require a simple answer? For instance, "What time will you be back in the office?"

Answer: "Well...I have to finish up this job. Then, I still have to check to see if the other job is ready for tomorrow. Then, I need to call Mark to see how he feels about changing the schedule for Friday. Before I do that, I should drive and see Steve on payment for the Thomas project... ." Notice that the question is still not answered.

I assure you if the person asking this question falls into the high D or C category, he would just about come unglued now. Not only impatient, but he is very likely livid if on a two-way radio without a way to cut to the chase. A simple answer – "5:30" – is all the information some people want.

This information is useful in any communication situation. Family, friends or social events will be handled more smoothly knowing their major DISC tendency. Imagine if this scenario were to take place between you and a potential client. We as the leaders of directors of events must conform to the tendencies of our prospects.

Let's take a close look, learn the DISC TENDENCIES and put them to use in our businesses.

D – Dominance	• Direct • Competitive • Confident **Primary Orientation: Results**
I – Influencing	• Friendly • Outgoing • Emotional **Primary Orientation: People**
S –Steadiness	• Sincere • Loyal • Good Listener **Primary Orientation: Cooperation**
C – Competency	• Analytical • By the Book • Cautious **Primary Orientation: Quality**

You can see how different we all are as individuals; yet, at the same time we are quite similar in these four tendencies. All people incorporate all four of these tendencies; however, it is the order in which they fall that makes us unique!

When one has actually taken the written test on this theory, it is quite an eye opener as to why we and others respond the way we do. For business purposes, it would certainly behoove us to know our prospect's "high" tendency, i.e., are they a high D, I, S or C?

It is somewhat easy to determine the high tendency and that's the important one. Don't bother yourself with being so scientific that you get a headache. Just attempt to find their "high" or "primary" tendency. We all have each of these tendencies to a certain extent. To find your order, you must take the actual test. These are standard tests at companies such as IBM, T. I. Rockwell, SAS and Glaxxo-Welcome, where they believe a person's personality must fit their profession.

The chart on the previous page shows the characteristics for each of the tendencies, and there are other traits to look for as well. For instance, a D would be very demanding, a "doer" and be very driven. When hearing these words and looking at the chart on D, if a certain someone comes into your mind, it is VERY likely that they are a high D.

The high I is a person who loves to talk. They are very inspiring and expressive. They are impulsive and generally caring. They can communicate their feelings and care about others. To sell something to this person, he has to feel good about you. (I should know. I am a high I.)

Then there is the S tendency. In addition to the chart,

some of the things to look for in an S would be the following. They like to feel safe and very secure. They are no risk-takers and they like things to be very stable and established. These groups usually make good friends because they are supportive and loyal.

The high C was put on the earth to pretty much drive the high I crazy. Look at the chart of the high C. This is pretty close to the opposite of I. The C is extremely logical, technical, calculated, needs a controlled schedule and is by the book. No surprises! DON'T make an unannounced sales call to a high C. This will ruin their schedule, interrupt their entire life and YOU will be sentenced to die.

Now you know all four of the tendencies. This knowledge can give you incredible sales niches just by interpreting your prospect.

HOW DO YOU DETERMINE ANOTHER'S STYLE?

What is your customer's detected behavior? Is it outgoing or reserved? If the observed behavior is outgoing, then we can be confident that they are either a high "D" or a high "I." Take a glance at your chart. If this person is a director or leader of others or focused on getting the results they want, then you have a high D! A person that is a "people person" tends to be very persuasive, likes to impress others and tends to be charismatic, is most definitely a high I.

If the observed behavior is reserved or introverted, then we know that they are either a high S or a high C. If they are more concerned with cooperating with others to complete a task and are very accepting of others, you probably have an S. Check your chart.

A person who takes his or her work seriously, believes it is absolutely important and must be done "just this way" with no deviation is a high C. So, with this priceless information, how do you communicate with the different styles?

DOMINANCE-
- Be direct, concise and to the point.
- Spare them the chitter chatter.
- They want a "what" answer, not a "how" answer.
- GET TO THE BOTTOM LINE.

INFLUENCING
- Spare the details.
- Socialize with the I.
- Follow up often.
- SHOW EXCITEMENT!

(As a high I, I feel that if you're not excited about what you are talking about, I am not going to be excited either.)

STEADINESS
- Start off slow and easy.
- Take time to acquire their trust.
- Answer all questions.
- Reassure them of the benefits safety and security.

COMPETENCY

- Provide proof.
- Testimonials and references are a must.
- Be prepared and perfectly structured.
- Answer the "how" question.
- Address any disadvantages early.

WHAT DO THE CUSTOMERS WANT?

DOMINANCE:

Remember a high D may want:

- Authority
- Challenges
- Prestige
- Freedom
- Varied activities
- Difficult assignments
- A logical approach
- An opportunity for advancement

Provide direct answers, be brief and to the point. Ask "what" questions, not how. Stick to business. Outline possibilities for the person to get results, solve problems and be in charge. Stress logic of ideas and approaches. When in agreement, agree with the facts and ideas, not the person. If timeliness or sanctions exist, get them into the open, but relate them to end results or goals.

INFLUENCING

Remember, a high I may want:

- Social recognition
- Popularity
- People to talk to
- Freedom of speech
- Freedom of control and detail
- Favorable working conditions
- Recognition of abilities to help others
- A chance to motivate people

Provide a favorable, friendly environment. Provide a chance for them to verbalize about people and their intuition. Provide ideas for transferring talk to action. Provide testimonials of experts on ideas. Provide time for stimulating and fun ideas. Provide details in writing, but don't dwell on it. Provide a democratic relationship. Provide incentives for taking on tasks.

STEADINESS

Remember, a high S may want:

- Status quo
- Security of situation
- Time to adjust
- Appreciation
- Identification with group
- Work pattern
- Limited territory
- Areas of specialization

Provide a sincere, personal and agreeable environment. Provide a sincere interest in them as a person. Ask "how" questions to get their opinions. Be patient in drawing out their goals. Present ideas or departures from status quo in a non-threatening manner. Give chance to adjust. Clearly define roles or goals and their place in the plan. Provide personal assurances of support. Emphasize how their actions will minimize their risk in a patient, persistent manner.

COMPETENCE:
Remember, a high C may want:
• Security
• No sudden changes
• Personal attention
• Little responsibility
• Exact job descriptions
• Controlled work environments
• Status quo
• Reassurance

Take time to prepare your case in advance. Provide straight pros and cons of ideas. Support ideas with accurate data. Provide reassurance that no surprises will occur. Provide exact job description with precise explanation of how it fits the big picture. If agreeing, be specific. If disagreeing, disagree with facts, not the person. Be prepared to provide many explanations.

Learn and use this valuable information in all your communication situations. It can save time and make you money. In your interactions with others, practice determining whether they are a D, I, S or C.

Remember to attempt and discuss issues in their style. This will make your conversation with them more understanding and pleasurable.

Keep in mind we are ALL involved in sales every day of our lives. The more pleasing and understanding we are, the more sense we make.

So with this, you can understand why you would approach a high I in an entirely different manner than you would a high D. Picture this: wouldn't we converse with a Marine drill sergeant a great deal differently than we would a drama teacher?

Enjoy the investigative work of determining one's style. Keep your eyes on the final objective of making the sale!

If your heart is in the right place, you will succeed. These facts will only help you get there a little quicker.

Success is a choice! You make it happen!

Chapter 13

How to Sell Your Business for Life

In Chapter 10, we learned the importance of knowing everything possible about our prospect prior to the first meeting. Remember how we compared it to a date, and we tried to anticipate the other's likes and dislikes? Preparing vigorously for the all-important night! The night that would ultimately determine does she really like me?

This is a situation we all can identify with, and it also proves the point that we all are salespeople. Most of us are involved in selling every day of our lives, even if we are just trying to sell our friends on OUR favorite restaurant for lunch!

Learning as much about your prospect as possible puts you in the role of "assistant buyer" or "consultant" if you are sincere about providing the best for your client. If you earn the customer's trust and they are comfortable with you, you become more of an educator and are not viewed as an opponent.

173

The sales call is a wonderful experience and challenge to those who do not fly by the seat of their pants! *"What do you mean – fly by the seat of my pants? I've been selling widgets for 12 years!"* Good. Those who have been selling the same product for a few years should have at least two valuable traits. One, they should be completely sold on their product or service with the utmost sincerity. (You cannot be convincing if YOU are not convinced.) Two, you cannot sell the same product year after year without hearing the same objections year after year. Take these objections and turn them into literally flawless reasons why a customer should buy.

Think diligently about your business a short time. Surely you have heard some of the same objections again and again. What are they? Start writing them down. The irony is the objections can be narrowed down to as few as six or seven.

We at HydroTech call them the "HydroTech Seven." This just means in our particular business as pressure cleaning contractors, we have narrowed down almost all objections to seven.

This small amount of knowledge practically gives a company a blank check to success. It's like taking a test in school when you are certain of what the questions will be. Think about it, when you were in school if you knew exactly what questions the professor was going to ask, you could ace *every* test! Why then as adults do we hear the same objections over and over, yet we continue to get stumped? Could it be we hear, but do not listen?

"THE HYDROTECH SEVEN"

If you are in the contract pressure cleaning business and I have put you to sleep, now would be a good time to wake up and start thinking. Get out your highlighter and learn to pay attention to the "old man's" answers. YOU WILL BE ANSWERING THESE QUESTIONS TO YOUR CUSTOMERS SOON! We are now entering "The HydroTech Seven." These are the seven most common questions our customers ask:

Q1. *"I am calling around to get bids on power washing my house. Could you come out and give me a price?"*

There it is plain and simple, the first question on your test! Your answer to this question and results are almost entirely up to you.

Our answer to this question, when asked by a homeowner would go something like this. While smiling, "Why yes ma'am. We would be happy to give you a price on the exterior cleaning of your house! We don't power wash though, we actually use a very gentle spray and mild solutions to deep clean the exterior of your home and protect the paint and surface. The machines just help us reach the heights and apply the soaps. I am sure it will exceed your expectations. It always does!"

This is answer part A to our first question. What we do here is separate ourselves from the "fly-by-nighters" who generally operate and survive the lifespan of a butterfly.

Customers generally reply, "OK, that sounds good. Can you send someone out to give me a price?"

Answer part B. "Actually, we can give you an exact price

right over the phone." (*Sound humble*) "However, if you are looking for the lowest price, Ms. Jones, I can almost guarantee we will be the highest price you get." (Tone of voice and voice inflection is crucial here. We will cover this in detail later in this series.)

One of two things will happen. You are a winner either way. The uncommon action is for the prospect to say, "OK, thank you very much" and hang up.

The second thing that might happen is for them to ask the question number 2.

Q2: *"Why are you so sure that you will be the highest?"*

Ninety-eight percent of the time this customer is sold, maybe 99 percent!

"Because we do not use labor hands, Ms. Jones. Our technicians are required to attend a four-day classroom and hands-on training program. They are then required to complete a rigorous three-month training program and pass a series of tests with a hundred percent accuracy on each test. They are then required to assist an instructor for their first month before being allowed to service your property alone.

"These technicians are able to troubleshoot a variety of stains on your home that may otherwise be left untouched. They can also speak with you intelligently on ways to better protect your home and alert you to any problems they may observe. Our technicians are trained to keep an eye out for anything they see that can help you be proactive in maintaining your home."

Note: HydroTech's questions and answers are a result of many years of hard labor, research and continuous development providing unsurpassed processes to our client base. Your answers would be different than ours unless you were operating under the same business ethics and educational requirements.

Q3: *"What kind of chemicals do you use?"*

"First, Ms. Jones, we don't use Clorox or bleach. Our chemist has found that bleach only contains 5.25 percent of the active ingredient for house cleaning and fungus control. We use this ingredient in its concentrated form along with cleaners that are used to target exterior stains as opposed to cleaning laundry.

"We also incorporate surfactants, surface acting agents, in our cleaners. This makes the cleaners stick to the surface kind of like shaving cream. The primary benefits of this are that it allows the chemicals to stick to the surface, penetrating the pores of the paint. This deep cleaning seeks out the spores of mold, mildew and other forms of non-vascular growth to completely eliminate them. This means your home will be cleaner much longer. Whereas bleach just bleaches the growth so it returns quickly since the spores are not terminated. It will look clean but only for a short time.

"The reason this occurs is because of the percentage of fungicide contained in bleach, 5.25 percent. In fact, even "over the counter" products you can purchase at paint stores, Home Depot and Lowe's may cost up to $8.00 a gallon, yet still only contain 5.25 percent. To make this worse, when a pressure washer performs a cleaning, they nearly all mix their solution 4 parts water to 1 part cleaner (4 gallons of water to 1 gallon of cleaner). This takes your 5.25 percent and brings it down to 1.05 percent, literally nonexistent.

Yet, it is usually taken a step farther. Most machines

operate on a down-stream injection system. These injection systems are set at the factory. They automatically introduce about 20 parts water to 1 part solution. So if we take their 1.05 percent active ingredient and deliver this through a 20 to 1 system, their cleaner is now at a .052 ratio. This means your home is not going to be cleaned to your expectations and so much contaminated water will have to be used, possibly damaging and killing plants.

Q4. *"Will it harm my plants and animals?"*

"Another advantage to using our concentrated housewash is that since the surfactants make it adhere to the wall like shaving cream, we only use a minute amount to clean your home. The product stays on the surface with no waste entering your soil system. Once cleaning is complete, your soil's pH level is guaranteed to be undisturbed. We not only use safe, environmentally-responsible solutions, but we also incorporate a complete neutralization or dilution process, again showing that we care about your home and foliage. Our solutions are 100 percent safe for pets, children, wildlife such as birds and even your favorite flowers or not so favorite weeds."

Q5. *"Are your chemicals environmentally friendly?"*

Contractors should not even try a "yes" without the knowledge and processes to back it up. How are they environmentally friendly? Use the term biodegradable and some educated person will call your bluff. A car is biodegradable, as is a chair and a pressure washer.

What are you REALLY telling your prospect? Take charge and get an educated edge. Become so educated on your solutions that it would take a chemist to fully understand the depths of your knowledge. Be the authority. Then speak simply with the confidence that if one needs to talk atoms and electrons you will still be the educated contractor that holds the answers as well as the client's confidence. (Another plug for our training course.)

Q6. *"Can you guarantee that mold and mildew will not come back?"*

"We guarantee it *will* come back! Our process will completely terminate 100 percent of the non-vascular growth on your home. This means it has to start the life cycle all over again. Just like when you clean your shower, it will return. The determining factor on the time of returned growth is completely dependent on the environment and process used for the termination and cleaning. Again, our penetrating surface acting agents carry concentrated solutions deep into the pores of the paint. This is the most effective process available in our industry."

Q7. *"Will your services streak my windows?"*

"We do gently spray your windows with our cleaners and follow with a hot rinse. This removes thick dust, dirt and pollen, but does not provide a squeaky clean appearance. If your windows are dirty, now they will be cleaner. However, if your windows are squeaky clean now, they may need to be cleaned after our process. The water in this area is pretty hard so sometimes there are water spots."

There are the questions to the test that you can be assured WILL BE ASKED, whether on a sales call or a phone call. These questions ARE in your future! You should have these answers so engraved in your brain that you could answer them under major anesthesia and a triple shot of tequila!

PRICE-DRIVEN MARKET?

So many contractors believe that exterior house cleaning is a totally price-driven market. NOT SO. Of course, if a prospect asks for the price and all you give them is the price, it is understandable how one could arrive at this conclusion. They may be price driven by the limited information they possess.

What is the prospect REALLY asking for? They don't know! I am reminded of the movie *Born Yesterday*. Melanie Griffith, a millionaire's pretty but terribly uneducated mistress, confides in her teacher that she doesn't need to be educated because she has everything she wants...a small TV to fit in her purse and a mink coat. Don Johnson, her savvy teacher, asks her, "How do you know you have everything you want if you don't know what else there is?"

Isn't this the same case with your customers? To most every homeowner prospect alive, all there is to know about cleaning their house is soap, bleach, a pressure washer and any uneducated imbecile that can start an engine for a couple of bucks. How do they know what they want if they don't know what else there is? To them, the only solid factor they know to go on is price.

Educating your prospects will be the challenge for you. So educate and become an assistant buyer. You will usually win whenever you can truly solve your customer's problems.

How To Use Voice Dynamics To Persuade The Client

I vividly remember the fist time I walked into the dojo (a karate school) with my bright new Gi (karate uniform). I was more nervous than a freshman on my first day at a new school. I had taken a few classes to see if I would like it, but this was the "big day"…the first official class of my two-year commitment.

I took a seat as the prior class was wrapping up their session. My classes up to that point had all been with beginners so I felt somewhat sportsman like; however, the class before me was overflowing with ballerina-like men and women. They jumped high, quick, smooth and elegantly. Gracefully, each landed light-footed with agility to make you wonder if this type of movement could ever be emulated without the special effects of TV.

I sat there in awe with enormous respect for those spectacular athletes. I then remembered I would have to share the same floor with some of those same "artists." I began to feel nauseous. The reality of my physical condition became crystal clear, at least compared to these gentle giants. I remembered how I felt like an overweight wino trying to walk a tightrope the night before at practice, and that was supposed to be the easy stuff. Intimidated was my name. Fear was my companion and retreat wanted to be my friend. Never have I felt so inadequate and out of place. Trembling inside, I was seriously considering the relationship with retreat thoughtfully.

Then a voice from the distance said "Hey mister. Is that your uniform?"

Sitting on a seat about four chairs down was a little boy with an innocent smile and feet swinging to and fro as his feet were not even close to the floor.

"It sure is," I said, thankful for the diversion from the intimidation of the class. "What's your name?" I asked.

"Nathan," he replied, "and I'm five years old."

I know it was probably kind of sneaky for me but I seized this opportunity to get a Brownie point. "Five! Wow, I would have guessed six or maybe seven!" His eyes lit up and he smiled so wide I think he could have eaten a banana sideways! "Do you take karate?" I asked.

"Yeah, I have a gold belt," he said.

Again the door was opened. I almost felt guilty. "NO WAY!" I replied in exaggerated disbelief. "I am not even a white belt yet. I bet you could teach me a lot." The smile got even bigger as his confidence glowed, and I had made a friend for life.

I had about 15 minutes before my class and I knew I would be reviewing some moves that we had supposedly learned from the night before. I did not have a clue. It was information overload. So I asked Nathan how to do this move, how to do that move, what is the name of the block that you do like this? Five-year-old Nathan answered every question and demonstrated every technique to the point I was actually remembering the moves and was looking forward to the class without feeling completely stupid.

Little Nathan was my teacher and my new friend. He pointed out his father in the group that was in session. He was a mirror image of little Nathan, except his moves were made with precision and the agility that emitted an air of confidence. His eyes met mine and he offered a friendly smile. I suddenly felt welcomed in this new environment.

I then saw the clock on the wall. My class was in five minutes and I still had to change! "Oh no, Nathan!" I said. "I have to hurry up or I will be late for my class."

I shook my little teacher's hand and thanked him for teaching me so much and hurried off to the locker room. I took my uniform out of its new package and was horrified by all of the strings. You don't see these strings when the uniform is on. Completely ignorant of where this is tied to where and this pulls through here and this tucks under there, I began to hyperventilate because the clock was ticking. Around the corner comes little Nathan.

"Nathan," I said in desperation, "do you know where all these strings are supposed to tie?"

"Sure, let me show you." He showed me one by one as his young voice assured me that I could do it and I was going to love my class. He loved the sport and with each statement he made, it was apparent that this young man was sold on karate. He was unbelievable. His enthusiasm was felt through the conviction of his voice. I was taking lessons, but

> "I studied the lives of great men and famous women; and I found that the men and women who got to the top were those who did the jobs they had in hand, with everything they had of energy, enthusiasm and hard work."
>
> – Harry Truman (1884-1972)
> 33rd U.S. President

the bottom line is that Nathan "sold" me on karate.

Reflecting on this incident, I can see how his use of voice, inflection and vocal variety played a lead role in my being "sold." A five-year-old expert in the use of vocal variety in sales? Of course not! However, as I have said so many times, when YOU are already sold on your product, the work is over. The rest is just fine-tuning. If YOU are not sold on your product or service, YOU will never be as effective as you could be when you truly believe in your heart that what you are offering your customer is the best! Therefore, "You can't be convincing if you are not convinced."

Psychologist Albert Meharbian states that we are FIVE times as likely to be influenced by voice than by spoken words alone when we listen to a speaker. If this is true, then we are more influenced by HOW a speaker talks, rather than what it is that the speaker actually says. A good speaking voice is loud enough to be heard, clear enough to be understood, expressive enough to be interesting and pleasing enough to be enjoyable. A good speaking voice should be a balance between extremes. These extremes are volume, pitch and rate, while having a pleasing sound quality.

These qualities come somewhat easy to some and take a lot of practice for others. Seasoned sales professionals understand the importance of vocal variety and record themselves rehearsing their sales pitch into a recorder until perfected.

Good examples of well-spoken words that you can almost be guaranteed of a good vocal variety are the words spoken by a grandmother or grandfather about their grandchildren. I enjoy listening to men who swear they could NEVER sell anything to anyone. In the next breath, their eyes light up, enthusiasm is gleaming from their entire body as they convince me of the uniqueness and intelligence of their grandson. The volume is a tad turned up. The pitch is consistent with the emotion of their stories, the rate is generally a little picked up because they are excited and the quality of voice is articulate because they don't want you to miss a word. Men and women who claimed they could not sell anything have sold me on many grandchildren!

I believe one of the most neglected areas in sales training is the use of your voice. One of the most significant things you can do to dramatically improve your sales and raise your profitability is to deliberately train your voice, learning how to use voice inflections. Most people do not even consider this part of their sales training. By their own experience or by accident, they usually develop it. What a tragedy – all the lost sales because of such a simple lack of training.

If you do not have your own digital recorder and are not recording your presentations, you are not becoming as much as you can become. Get yourself a good recording device. It will help you become more articulate and much more confident! Don't just contemplate, "Hey, that's a good idea." *Do it!*

If you want to improve on anything, YOU have to take action. Knowledge is *not* power. Knowledge is *potential* power. It becomes powerful the moment YOU take action.

Once you have the equipment, listen back and analyze your presentation. Then, script your presentation and practice addressing every objection conceivable.

Remember the "HydroTech Seven?" The way you close the sale, your opening statement, the transition from educating the customer to giving them the opportunity to use your service. Give it everything you've got. Do it as you normally would do! You will discover some incredible information in your recordings. Some delightful, some impressive, some embarrassing and some information you will not be happy to hear at all, except for the fact that it will help you become infinitely more professional. Isn't that what it's all about anyway?

One thing I have discovered is that most sales professionals who own their own businesses talk too much. (Me too.) I think the reason is because we are proud of our businesses. However, we must keep in mind that the customer is not impressed by our accomplishments. They only want to know what we can do for them.

I have also discovered that most businessmen and women tend to get into a monotone rut toward the end of their presentation. You will also learn that you talk about a number of things that have absolutely nothing to do with the sale at all!

When you put the words to script, they are going to remind you of so much you have forgotten. Write down those points, those examples, those ideas, and when you write down what you have been using along with what you have forgotten, some awesome new ideas are going to be generated from this assignment. You are going to realize that you are much farther down the path of professional sales and pressure-cleaning entrepreneur than you originally thought you were.

Now you need to start training your voice so that you can make it more effective. You can change word meaning by voice inflection. You can ask your child to do something, or you can ask a prospect to do something and it can either be in love or hate, using the same words. The tone and the inflection of the voice are what makes the difference. Remember what your mom used to say, "It's not what you said, it was the way you said it." (Just before your dad smacked your head off.)

Practice this and re-record the sentence, "I did not say he ate mom's chicken." You should be able to use voice inflection to form this sentence to mean at least seven different meanings. Think now. Don't just give up! Anything we do requires effort.

The niche we have is that customers *need* our service. Keep the clients' needs at the forefront of your actions. Doing what is right will never lead us astray. Eliminate your competition! Convince your prospects, give 100 percent, be accountable for your actions and acquire a reputation for life.

Consider every dispute as a potential bad mark, even if the disputes are with bozos. If you have read this far, I believe in you. The "get rich quick" boys and girls have bailed by now. This type of improvement requires real work and serious action. That means YOU are probably the real deal. The real deal is what our industry needs. Honesty, integrity and accountability; these are the characteristics of success.

I encourage you to practice these traits and move mountains in our industry. Rock the world with your excellence. I believe in you. YOU believe in you, even when others don't. Success is a choice! Make the choice and soar! You have the power and you can make it happen.

EDUCATION IS NEVER ENDING!

To echo what we have recently determined about the sales call, you have to believe in yourself and your service of product! You accomplish this by learning, researching, role playing and becoming an authority on your service. Once an authority, you will know in your heart, as well as your mind, that what you are offering is truly in the prospect's best interest. This enthusiasm and confidence will be transferred into the prospect's mind and heart as well.

Again, selling is transference of feelings whether on a face-to-face sales call or on the phone. If I can make you feel about my product of services the way I feel about my product or services, you will literally break your neck to obtain my goods, therefore maintaining those feelings!

What if I am not an authority? What if I know there is someone else who will do a better job? I *now* need to make a choice: get myself in gear and bury my head in the books, education materials and role models, or find another area where I will be able to exceed my customers' expectations. Why? Because if I am not sold, I cannot sincerely sell you. Remember the transference of feelings. You cannot be convincing if you are not convinced! I'm not talking hooray rallies and positive thinking. I am talking about providing your customers with hard core, sound solutions to their problems.

Once your homework is done and you have a passion for what you are doing, you in no way have to be concerned with "selling" again. Confident in your abilities with the knowledge in your heart and your head, you can proceed to stop taking "sales calls" and begin taking calls in which you are simply educating the customer. This takes all the pressure off you. As opposed to being drilled by a prospect, you can now relax and educate them on the facts of your service.

Then kindly place the ball back in their court and wait for another question *or* the order.

Prospects Buy You!

The primary point you need to consider is that before people buy your goods or services of any substantial value, they absolutely must be sold on you. No matter if you bought this book or it is part of your training curriculum with ANY training school, in order to build a sales career, you need a rock solid foundation on which you can build your business and reputation. That is what I am talking about throughout this series. People need to know that they will not be disappointed if they buy from you. Establishing trust can be as quick as the first meeting or take as long as three, four or five years. However, it can be lost within the blink of an eye. Weigh all of your decisions with truth and the long-term consequences in mind.

A sale begins the moment the phone rings or you impact a prospect. The persona of whoever answers the phone becomes the company's identity. Every characteristic a customer visualizes of your business will be built upon the honesty spoken here. The person answering the phone, just as the salesperson, has a critical role. He or she is the heart of the business. This individual *cannot* have a bad day. This person must be motivated and smiling or sent home. The first impression cannot be jeopardized by ho-hum attitudes. The phone should always be answered with a big smile! Put a mirror on your desk, or if need be, a picture of your mother-in-law with a drawn-in moustache and blackened-out teeth.

Whatever makes you laugh. Because, that attitude will be felt through miles of phone wire and most likely put a smile right on the recipient's face too.

The tone of voice, pitch, energy, dynamics and enthusiasm will most always reflect right back to you from the prospect! This also makes you fun and pleasant to talk to so the customer will delight in the conversation. At this time, endorphins – chemicals released from the brain that produce pleasure – are being introduced into their system and often yours. This makes them feel good and also helps eliminate the barrier of sales person vs. prospect roles.

In almost every study, individuals respond in accordance to how they perceive the individual initiating the conversation. Imagine your prospect as a large mirror. Your smile, attitude, energy, enthusiasm, politeness and professionalism will all reflect right back at you. In contrast, a ho-hum, thumb-sucker attitude will come back twice as fast with triple force. The beauty is that YOU are in control of the direction and level of the conversation! This is your ace in the hole.

YOU HOLD THE POWER!

You have the power to determine the mood and direction of almost all of your interactions both in person and on the phone, both socially and professionally. I challenge you to put this exercise to the test! You will be amazed!

The next time someone asks you how you are doing,

give him or her a big grin and say "I am doing great, but getting better! How in the world are you doing?" I assure you a smile will follow, and the mood for conversation will be set in a light of fun, humor and a stress-free environment. In comparison, if someone asks "how are you doing," look stressed and say "All right, getting by or hanging in there." Watch and feel the weight of their reaction and emotions as you have set the stage for a bland, dead-end conversation with nowhere positive to go. Yes, you are in control. You determine the mood of the sales call, phone call or any personal interaction. You determine how you are accepted at a social event. You determine the tone and setting for your interviews. You hold the power!

REACT OR RESPOND?

You cannot change your circumstances; however, you do have the ability to control how you handle the circumstances. Do you react or respond?

Reaction is not usually a good thing. When we react, it is usually as a defense. Pretend you go to the doctor and he says, "We are going to have to change your medicine because your body is reacting to the medication." This is not what you want. However, imagine he says, "Your body is responding wonderfully to the medication." This means you are going to get well! So what will it be? React or respond?

If you must react, I highly recommend that you react in a manner in which Chuck Swindoll describes: *The longer I live, the more I realize the impact of attitude on life. Attitude, to me, is more important than facts. It is more important than the past, than education, than money, than circumstances, than failures, than successes, than what other people think or say or do. It is more important than appearance, giftedness or skill. It will make or break a company, a church and a home. The remarkable thing is we have a choice every day regarding the attitude we will embrace for that day. We cannot change our past. We cannot change the fact that people will act in a certain way. We cannot change the inevitable. The only thing we can do is play the one string we have, and that is attitude. I am convinced that life is 10 percent what happens to me and 90 percent how I react to it. And so it is with you. We are in charge of our own attitudes."*

Your response is a choice. I challenge you to choose to respond in an uplifting manner! When someone asks how you are doing, do they really care? No, not usually. So use this as an opportunity to energize someone's life, give humor and kindness, provide people with hope, love, joy and sincerity and watch their reflections enrich your life each time you make this effort! Besides, if you learn to love the sale, you will not even consider it as work. You will consider it a *living*!

Here is a checklist to develop a great sales call procedure:

• You know *your* business must be built on a foundation of trust.

• You are continuously learning while becoming *the* authority in your industry in your area.

• You have written down all of your prospect's commonly asked questions.

• You are learning everything possible about your

prospect.

• You can recite the answers to the commonly asked questions in a beautiful, logical, educated and elocutionary manner.

A Little More Magic

The secret to making the sales call is not really a secret; it's more of the "magic" of marketing. It is the inner belief that you have for your product or services along with providing your customer with the truth, even if it means sending them somewhere else.

Education, knowledge, belief in the product or service, homework about the prospect and a smooth delivery are all important. However, as taught to me by my friend and role model Zig Zigler, "Steve, they will never care how much you know, *until* they know how much you care."

What Does The Customer Want?

Let's take a moment and explore the needs and demands of the corporate customer. What needs do they have that must be filled? Corporate accounts are residual. You make the sale one time and make unsurpassed customer service a way of life – every day.

Excuses will not work in a corporate structure. No

matter what the problem, the job must be done on time. Systems must be employed in case someone drops the ball. There must be someone else ready to carry that ball to the completion of the game. If a truck or unit breaks down, or an employee is sick, the job must go on. In the corporate world, time doesn't stand still because one player is injured. There is too much money at stake. The corporate accounts are tough. They are not for anyone in this business that cannot focus day in, day out, and years down the road.

A residual corporate account in any industry can streamline your business to security. For modest financial reasons, let's look at one: the building industry. This approach can be your security to the next level in business. You be the judge. Take one building corporate account that builds 600 houses per year and multiply the package price.

Ex. 600 houses per year

x 450 dollars

$270,000

That is $270,000 per year...*every* year. No resells. No more ads. Just knock their socks off every single day with uncompromising customer service.

It just so happens that I am fortunate enough to have one particular corporate account with the magic. As a result of many years of mutual respect, the roots of our companies grow stronger together.

Chapter *14*

arketing the asses

Imagine, if you will, driving down your favorite countryside in the car of your dreams. What color is it? How fast are you going? Imagine every detail of the vehicle down to the smell of the new leather interior. What are you wearing? Are you casual or dressed to the max?

You pull your dream ride onto your property and what do you see? Remember, this is your dream so make it perfect. Is the land plush with a lengthy driveway, manicured landscaping and a colossal grand entrance?

Envision the home. Is it a mansion or a log cabin? Supply your home with every detail you have always wanted. The kitchen, the huge walk-in pantries, the private, organized workshop with all the tools you have been wishing you had. The garage is so neat and large that you actually have room for the cars and truck without tripping over the junk you have been collecting for Goodwill for the last six months!

The huge master bedroom and the great room are so big you would have to buy a riding vacuum cleaner. You have your own walk-in closet that is really yours and not overtaken by your spouse. You actually have a separate closet as large as a bedroom designed exclusively for ladies' shoes. Everything is always in its place, and your life is free from any money worries. Life is good.

Now, if you will, come back to reality. Hopefully, it wasn't too much of a descent. Why is it that you are not where you want to be financially and experiencing the benefits of success?

Winners take action while losers make excuses, so be careful with your answer. Now that you have had a wake-up call as to where you want to be and where you actually are, what can you do to modify your reality? Honestly, putting some of the following ideas into action may change your complete financial health, resulting in an overall more rewarding life.

How Do I Make The BIG Money?

To our own demise, we often spend hours attempting to convince a prospect to spend a couple of thousand dollars. Consider an alternative. Marketing the masses.

Consider marketing your product or service to a large group of your targeted market. When you fine-tune your audience, you have before you groups of people who are all in need of your product or service!

It is documented that the public's number one fear is speaking to a large group of people. I kid you not! The public's second most feared situation is death. If you can overcome the obstacles, you may very well be on the path to the dream you were just creating!

Case in point. If you spend a couple hours planning a proposal for restoring and preserving a cedar roof and are granted the job, that is good. This project would average a strong $4000. However, what if we marketed the masses and concentrated on homeowner associations? A typical town home community with 50 homes makes for an average homeowners' association (HOA). Therefore, HOAs are dramatically more profitable. Four-thousand dollars for each of the 50 roofs totals $200,000. It is common for associations to have money budgeted and available for such services or even take out loans from financial institutions.

Don't limit yourself to homeowners' associations. There are multitudes of organizations that need your product or service. Allow me to get your imagination flowing. Most every city has an apartment association, often more than one.

For our example, let's use the "Chicago Apartment Association." A presentation to this group would often reach hundreds of decision makers. What is even more priceless, you become the authority in your field depending on your professionalism. The financial return on such a presentation is likely to be overwhelming.

Since apartment managers are generally responsible for many buildings, the buildings are usually cleaned in phases. Ten buildings this week, 10 buildings next week, 10 the week after and so on. Consider only one proposal accepted out of 100 prospects in your ONE presentation. A complex with 30 buildings turns into a whopping $35,000 in three weeks of work with one helper.

Take into consideration this is a modest case scenario.

Nearly anyone would close more than one percent.

You will find one homebuilders' association in every average-sized city. Spend 30 minutes in front of the local association and I will just about guarantee you are the only person in your industry that has ever spoken to them on this level. Results? Credibility and exposure have authority.

The targeted builder in our market brings in $24,000 a year to our company. Experience has shown us that *each* presentation is worth at least eight new contractors. The math? Eight times $24,000 is an additional $192,000 a year.

I will give you one more example to provoke your curiosity and prove my point – Building Owners and Managers Association (BOMA). This association is compiled of the owners and managers of rental homes, shopping centers, shopping malls, office buildings and office parks. One presentation to this group and you could be well on your way to the dream.

I will be very conservative and suggest you land only one account. However, this account manages 20 shopping centers. Twenty centers multiplied by the average concrete cleaning of their sidewalks and parking garages is $2,000 each. That's $40,000 for a one-time cleaning! You provide them with quarterly service on each property. (The upper-scale centers require a maintenance program.) This brings your company an additional $160,000 per year, *every* year as long as you maintain "the magic."

Finding your targeted audience is simple. Most associations meet at least once a quarter. Getting the time to provide them with a presentation is not difficult. What holds most of the "would-be" wealthy business people back is that number-one fear of public speaking.

Let me share some tips and tricks that I have learned from some of the best speakers in the world. While you may be reluctant to picture yourself speaking to a crowd of prospects, let us reflect back to our dream and back to the $587,000 that we could have perhaps generated in only four well-prepared professional sales presentations as we just illustrated!

DETERMINE YOUR MARKET

Back to the basics, *targeting your market and maintaining focus* is one of the primary challenges for marketing the masses, especially when there is so much to clean!

Prospects want a professional in their area of specialization. What do you do? If your answer to a prospect is "everything," you are likely to be regarded as a "handyman." The alternative answer, although it may be true, may be just as fatal. "We clean tractor trailers, vent hoods, houses, decks, driveways, a little new construction clean up, heavy equipment here and there… yada, yada, yada." Most people involved in this industry are aware of the necessity to be somewhat diversified. However, your prospect wants *the* authority. Discover your prospect's *focus* and fine-tune your entire presentation around *that*.

It's difficult when marketing to limit your company to one specialization. You may do several equally well. Often, service companies overwhelm a prospect by creating brochures that list all of their services. It is difficult for an industrial prospect to imagine someone who cleans houses to have the power, equipment and know-how to clean around million-dollar robotics in a factory environment. (They link the house washers to cases of bleach and a $75 rental unit.)

The opposite also applies. Ms. Homeowner reads of your high-capacity, high-heat and high-pressure capabilities. She envisions the paint practically melting off wood as the dynamic water force blasts her windows out of the frames!

It is imperative to focus our marketing efforts directly at our targets. If in fact we do provide house washing and other residential applications, we should use terminology that will fall pleasantly on the ears of homeowners. "Soft, gentle spray, mild detergents, environmentally friendly, safe and effective, with proven results." This is music to the homeowner's ears.

I recommend one marketing strategy for homeowners and a completely different approach for each division or process. Industrial, commercial, restoration, real estate and other special services should have their own identity. Yes, this means additional costs in marketing materials. However, when you are face-to-face with the BIG contracts, the service in question is not an "add-on" service. It is *your* specialty. Don't be concerned about missed work by being clearly focused on ONE service at a time. If you are performing a focused application and are asked about exterior home cleaning, you don't miss a sale. You just reply "Oh yes, that is our residential division. That is a completely different process. Would you like information on those services?" This position allows you to remain true to the specialization you are now providing as well as freedom to change directions, as a customer's needs change.

Flexibility is the key to success in this industry and for

most all service businesses. Being able to transition from one specialty to the other as the needs of customers arise is not difficult. What may be tricky is the ability to redirect your thinking, mind set and terminology from one specialty in the morning, new construction, to an opposite specialty in the afternoon, home washing. The customer is watching the same company, but they know it is a completely different process.

Focus Again

If we chase two rabbits at a time, they will both get away. So let's set our sights on one, property management.

You decide on this specialty because it is residual money, a high profit margin and you enjoy the scope of the work. You are a bit hesitant to take on an entire association for your first presentation, so you decide to start small.

Often, property management companies specialize in one type of property management with numerous property managers; for instance, outside strip malls and shopping centers. These managers are usually required to attend weekly or monthly meetings together. Fortunately for us, there is usually one poor soul with the responsibility of creating the agenda for each meeting. More times than not, they are desperate for something new and fresh to bring life back to the ho-hum, trivial meetings.

You can be the answer! DO YOUR HOMEWORK! Get a good edge by learning as much as you can about the NEEDS of your audience. KNOW YOUR AUDIENCE. It is easier to talk to someone you know and understand. You can base your points on common knowledge and shared beliefs. What is their point of view? What are the problems THEY face? What makes them tick? What is THEIR terminology? What are their ages, sex, education level and cultural background? How many managers will be attending? How can you solve their problems and make THEM successful?

Continue to do informal research up to the minute before your presentation. The depth of your research could possibly take you from the "outsider" role to an "insider" role. It is always easier to work from the inside. This means you are viewed as one of the team members.

While on this assignment, saturate yourself in total property management research. Isolate your total focus on how you can beautify and aid in the success of each property. Get to know the store owners and their concerns. Find the solutions to problems before your presentation. Be prepared to identify ongoing problems with immediate solutions.

You may be arranging to speak to 15 property managers. One property manager could spend more money with you in one month than most people make in a year. Make the sale once. Keep the customer for a lifetime. Build your business. DO NOT DEVIATE from your target. Put this plan of action to work. Research and hone in to make the big sales. This plan is a funny little plan – it will absolutely work…if YOU do. Take the challenge to boost your sales. Start your research NOW. Take the step to change your entire financial health. Get busy and get this portion behind you.

We will continue with our research into the next section titled "Effective Presentations." Meanwhile, live as though it were impossible to fail. Your mind was designed for success!

Chapter 15

Effective Business Presentations

FIVE HUNDRED, EIGHTY-SEVEN THOUSAND DOLLARS is how much money we generated in only four hypothetical presentations in the last section. "Marketing the Masses" was proven to be a truly effective way to multiply your marketing efforts. We demonstrated how speaking to many clients with the same needs at one time is far more effective and profitable than reaching them one by one. It also establishes you as the authority.

Chances are no one else in your industry has the professionalism to speak to their group on this level, or worse, has the ability and does nothing. Always remember that doing nothing is a conscious or unconscious decision to fail. It is not the Einsteins with the PhDs that I see succeeding; it is the good old boys that will not give up, that keep getting up every time they get knocked down. Over, over and over they fail, fall or get pulled down by people, circumstances or disasters. These are the ones that I see on top in the long run. These are the ones that make their own success and always come back no matter how hard the hit. *Real courage is the ability to face your fears.*

If the reality of speaking to a group of executives makes you tremble, good. You have an opportunity to change your life completely by facing that fear and gaining all the benefits that this fear has denied you until now. We are talking more than just financial gain now. What growth does one have if the act of speaking in public does not scare them silly? However, when we face our fears, we learn, grow and become better as a result of our triumphs.

We learn so much by facing our fears. First, we learn that the fight is really not against what we are frightened of; the fight is with ourselves. If you have no fear of speaking to a large group, then this section may help bring you prosperity. If you do have a fear, then this section may not only bring prosperity but also be the beginning of a turning point in your life.

Where do I start? A review from the last section shows us that first we must *define our objectives*. Who is it we want to sell? In order to continue to move smoothly, let's use property managers as our target audience. Our objective should be to speak to as many decision-makers as possible. Educate them on how your services will save them money, make them money, and make them look good to their superiors and their tenants and also make their job easier. Final objective, make the sale.

KNOW THY AUDIENCE

Get personal. What are the customer's needs? Finding out all of this information takes research and hard work.

What is their terminology? What are the problems they face daily? Do you really care? If not, find another market. You won't fake it!

How can *you* solve their problems? How will you make them a success? They want to know what is in it for *them*.

If your customers are property managers for shopping centers, study each of their properties thoroughly, taking notes on each solution you find to a problem. Meet informally with each tenant. Find out what their needs and concerns are. Is there a problem with the service they are receiving? If so, document this problem, find a solution and present your solution to your audience as "normal procedure" and make it that way. A happy tenant is a property manager's dream!

Be prepared to identify ongoing problems with immediate solutions. This type of research requires intense focus on the property management field, just as did other targeted markets when you solicited their accounts.

I am confident if you saturate yourself in all kinds of property management publications and take enough of the property managers, superintendents and assistants to lunch, you will start using their terminology. You will begin to think like a property manager, at which point, you are one of them.

People always prefer to do business with those they feel comfortable with. When speaking to a group of builders, do just as much homework.

A few years ago, I put together sales and customer service material to train all the salespeople for the CARQUEST Corporation. I was not familiar with their day-to-day problems and industry terminology. For me to be successful and accepted as an authority, I had to learn their business inside and out; just as you will need to learn everything about your clients.

Learn *their* terminology, problems, solutions and what makes them tick. How do they dress? What do they drive? What do they all have in common that you can relate to? What do they think is funny? Who are the real movers and shakers in the audience going to be?

Use this same approach to every industry you are planning to market. If you do this research and KNOW your audience before you ever take the podium, you will have the number one defense against the nervousness that will come your way. Knowledge is your best defense! No matter what targeted group you address, KNOW THY AUDIENCE!

DEVELOPING YOUR PRESENTATION

*W*hat are you trying to accomplish with this *presentation?* Write a clear and concise presentation purpose statement summarizing in one sentence what you want to do to produce what results. This can be exactly the same as *define your objectives*, just in simple sentence form.

With this down, you can remain focused on *this* target. You are about to spend a lot of time and effort preparing your presentation, and your audience will go out of their way to hear what you have to say. So it makes sense to stay on track and spend some time up front to assure all this hard work and time pay off.

Brainstorm and write down why this talk is important to this audience. How will they benefit? What's in it for them? Visualize what will happen as a result of your talk. What do you want them to do? Describe the results in clear, measurable terms.

I usually visualize the clients scheduling several jobs on residual contracts. Just one or two convinced property managers could schedule $100,000 per year. Every year!

This motivates me to work very hard on my presentations. Compare your talk to a music concert. All the hard work is done in practice after practice, then multiple rehearsals. However, payday is the concert, and that's a piece of cake!

Many professions are paid in this way. Ninety-five percent of the work done for a boxing champion is done outside of the ring. The ice skater has put in hundreds of hours for a two-minute performance. The gymnast, the dancer, the basketball team, the lawyer, the teacher, the surgeon, the writer, the actress – so many professions' successes are determined by the hard work put in behind the scenes. Get off on the right foot. *Work hard!*

The following is to serve as a basic analysis of what you are trying to accomplish. (You should answer these questions for yourself.) It is important to know *exactly* what you want. This way you can spend all of your time focused on the outcome and stay on track. Below is an example:

1. Why is this presentation important?

• **To the audience?** Property managers have a real need for someone who can take charge, problem solve, remove gum, graffiti, rust, oil, fats, etc., without flooding their tenants' stores, streaking their windows and interrupting their tenants' businesses.

• **To me?** This presentation is an opportunity to establish myself as the authority in this industry to all that attend. It will also be a major step in overcoming my fear of speaking in public.

2. What will happen as a result?

• *For the audience?* A successful presentation will mean a higher occupancy rate for the property managers who use our service: more money, cleaner properties, less stress for managers, better relations with tenants and the new condition and orderliness of their properties impress their superiors!

• *For me?* If I contract with only two of the managers in the audience, that means a residual $100,000 a year as long as we maintain our standards and promote good public relations with the company, the property managers and their tenants!

PREPARING AND REHEARSING YOUR PRESENTATION

Now we want to turn our objectives into a presentation. Narrow your objectives into three. This will get you focused and get your creative juices flowing.

For example, if I were going to give a presentation on the relevance of the Biblical story "David and Goliath," my objectives may look something like this:

• Create excitement among the audience for this and other Bible studies.

• Make sure the audience understands and retains the reading of David and Goliath as a lesson on perseverance and determination.

• Teach the audience in the notion of "interpretation" and what it means to them.

• Close with them having an understanding of why many other stories in the Bible mean something to them.

Your time allotment will determine the depth of your presentation. The more time you have, the more detailed you can be. In a sales presentation, my experience is to *be fast* and *be in demand*. Create excitement; get them interested and creative in all the possibilities for *their* success. Tell them just enough to generate their imagination and move on. *Leave them wanting more.*

Never overstay or let a presentation drag on and on with questions and answers. This is a tremendous letdown and an awful way to fizzle out. If you do have a question and answer session, limit it to 15 minutes. Politely announce that you *must* limit your time to maintain your schedule.

Never end with the question and answer forum. If there are questions and answers at the end of my rehearsed presentation, I plan for it and regain control of the audience. Turn their attention back to the objectives by restating the benefits to them and try to leave them on the highest note they will be on that day: a story, a quote, a relevant true success story and an encouraging word.

Being in demand here in the view of all their associates is a good time to set a few meetings one-on-one in the back of the room. Some will be chomping at the bit to talk to you; these are the ones to set appointments with.

Leave as soon as possible. You will be in high demand. Remember, human nature makes us want what we can't have. Give your phone numbers, get theirs and e-mail addresses, but politely get out while you are still in high demand.

PRACTICE, PRACTICE, PRACTICE

K nowing your subject is your insurance policy. You may not be a professional speaker; however, if you know your stuff and your presentation, you will be respected.

The single most critical step in your presentation is rehearsal. A great presenter always appears to be at ease, relaxed, comfortable and in control. Demeanor is not the result of natural poise. This is the result of effective rehearsals. Here are some helpful suggestions for rehearsal.

Steve's Steps for Successful Rehearsal

• Use 3 x 5 note cards of your key points, times and directions while rehearsing.

• Videotape practice sessions. Study your expressions, gestures and tone of voice.

• Rehearse in front of family, friends and associates. Get feedback. This is not the time to be shy or too cool to be a learner. Save that for when you make the big sales and take those who supported you to a special dinner. They deserve it.

• Rehearse with the equipment you will be using. A pointer, a slide projector, overheads, videos or the "Old Faithful" flip chart.

• Sit in the room and get "at home" in the room where you will be speaking.

• Your face is an instrument. Assure your expressions are in sync with your words.

• Practice smiling naturally. A fake or insincere smile is a real turnoff.

Bye-Bye Butterflies!

Again, knowing that you have done your homework and are well prepared will provide you with the peaceful confidence that will kick in soon after you begin to speak. Get the audience involved quickly; they like it and it takes some of the attention off of you. Complete preparation equals total confidence. Prepare, then rehearse until you can give your presentation with no "ahs," "ums" or other verbal no-no's. Be yourself! Don't try to be Tony Robbins or Robin Williams.

The First 180 Seconds

This is the scene: you are about to step up to the podium to deliver a 20-minute sales presentation. The audience is made up of 50 knowledgeable professionals that could easily write your check to prosperity. The beginning of your presentation is slightly like flying an airplane...take-off is the most critical phase. If the audience does not buy in now, you will be trying not to crash the entire presentation.

What you need is a guaranteed way to grab the audience's attention for the first 180 seconds! The first impression you give to your listeners is a lasting one. This is the time to win them over. They are deciding if you like them and if they like you, and they are wondering if you are worth listening to.

Most everyone's attention is at its peak for the first 180 seconds. Much of this time is spent just sizing you up. Take advantage of their utmost attention, be creative and *keep it*!

Some helpful ideas are to make your audience your friend by showing respect and building rapport. Prove you respect their time by being incredibly prepared. Empathize with them, show commonality and communicate similar interest. This is where all the homework comes in handy because you are communicating with them in their language. We all like people who are like us.

Use your eyes to make contact with as many individuals as possible as often as possible. Eye contact is a good attention grabber. The second you take the stage, *grab* their attention and run with it! Be creative! Use quotes, stories, trivia, music, immediate benefits, humorous situations, real world situations, current events or even give something away, but most of all, make it relevant!

I don't recommend starting off a presentation with "Good morning (afternoon, evening), ladies and gentlemen," yada, yada, yada. That is so boring. Open with a line that grabs attention. It doesn't have to be outrageous, just attention grabbing. Get the listeners involved even if it is just to raise their hands

> ## "Everyone has butterflies in their stomach. The only difference is the pros have their butterflies to fly in formation."
> – Zig Ziglar

or answer a question.

Seven percent of our presentation result is contingent on your words, 38 percent on your tonality and dynamics of your voice, and 55 percent on your body language. It isn't just what you say, but *how* you say it. Ninety-three percent of your outcome is determined by non-verbal messages.

Rehearse your presentation, and when you know it so well you can watch *yourself* on video and feel confident, then you are ready. Believe in your product or service because this will be screaming from your non-verbal communication.

This information properly applied is enough to keep you busy on the path to success! Before we continue with more, I encourage you to take action now. Take a little step at a time and when you look back, you will have traveled miles!

> "The paradox faced by every presenter is that it takes considerable preparation in order to be spontaneous."
>
> – Bob Gerold

Success comes when you take responsibility for yourself. Responsibility is the knowledge you are personally accountable for all the activities in which you are associated. It is the urge to do or get done what ought to be done. Waiting on Santa Claus, luck, an inheritance or someone else to solve your problems is a sign of stagnation. Believing in personal responsibility in your own life is necessary for security and happiness.

Effective presentations and your financial wealth are almost completely determined by your will to take action and *do*! Face your fears knowing that the fear really isn't the darkness, heights, water or even public speaking. As you pursue this journey to financial freedom, don't forget to live every moment.

Life is not just the moment you deposit your first million dollars! Life is what you are doing *right now*. It is the joy of the dream, the pursuit of growing and the actions of the process.

The fear is within you, so the fight is with yourself. The fight is to succeed, knowing you are never defeated until you stop taking action and quit. So never, ever quit. This is your guarantee. You *will* achieve greatness.

How to Create Profitable Presentations

> *"People will pay more to be entertained than educated."*
>
> — *Johnny Carson*

This is a fact that is ever so true in our industry. I have been to convention after convention and observed so-called entrepreneurs make rude comments about the price of a 20- to 40-dollar guidebook or manual that could save them thousands of dollars in trial and error. Yet hours later, the same bodies are the big spenders at the bar or restaurant, far exceeding the cost of the publication. Are these folks really entrepreneurs or just lost souls searching for a place to belong? Both, I think.

Over the years, some have come around while others have just disappeared. The ones that disappear are the same ones that elect to ignore this type of strategic marketing. "That's not for me," they say. "I would never try to sell to a large group of people. I am more comfortable just putting flyers on a mailbox." These excuses may be the truth, but *no lions are caught in mousetraps.* To catch lions you have to think in terms of *lions*, not in terms of mice!

Your mind is always creating one kind of trap or another. What you catch determines on the kind of thinking you do. "It is your thinking that attracts to you what you will receive" (Thomas Dreier). You must make a habit of succeeding! You must have a will to succeed! But what is more important is the *will* to prepare! It's the will to preserve and practice 'til it's nearly mundane!

Spectacular achievement is almost always preceded by unspectacular preparation! Let's get busy and continue on with our game plan. You are a doer. The dreamer will still be sleeping long into your transition into financial stability! As a doer, you are now ready for the next step in preparing your presentation.

MORE MONEY!

FIVE HUNDRED, EIGHTY THOUSAND DOLLARS was our earnings after four hypothetical presentations. This is a motivating factor for me to pursue this form of marketing. Presenting to the companies with large budgets builds longtime security.

We established that the first 180 seconds are crucial in gaining you prospect's attention in the form of an audience. The average person has an attention span of five or six minutes. You MUST manage your presentation in a way that gets your point across and keeps your clients at the highest possible point of interest.

Audiences need a dose of business entertainment to keep them alert. Give them booster shots throughout your presentation to keep them interested!

Presentation Facts to Keep Interest

- **People think four times faster than they speak.** (Except in my hometown of Raleigh, NC, and I have heard also in West Virginia.)
- **Hook your audience by building rapport.** Show them you value their time by letting them know where you are headed.
- **Establish and maintain eye contact.** Be generous with sincere smiles.
- **Know the client's natural highs and lows.** The first 180 seconds (high), the moment you mention "in closing" (high), the middle is up to you.
- **Maintain excitement** by including business entertainment every five to six minutes or more. Remember, make it relevant and *be yourself*!
- **Be creative, be different, and be memorable.** Ideas for crowd pleasers are fun!
- **Music! Games! Jokes! Stories! Activities! Questions!**
- **Free Giveaways.**

A young man is sentenced to 25 years in prison and on his first day in the cell, he hears someone down the cellblock yell out, "22!" Everyone within earshot, including his new cellmate, laughs hysterically until their sides hurt and their eyes are watering.

A few minutes later someone yells out "86!" Again, the prison is just filled with uncontrollable laughter everywhere. Feeling left out and confused, the young man asked his cellmate,"What's all that about?"

"Well, we have all been here so long we numbered all our jokes," said the old timer. "That way, instead of tellin' the whole joke, we can just holler out the number when we want a good laugh."

Being a congenial young man and eager to make new friends, the young prisoner yells out "22!" Not a prisoner laughs. He then tries again, "87!" Nothing. Then again, "48!" Dead cold silence.

Wounded and embarrassed, he turns to his cellmate and asks what went wrong. The wise old timer looks at him, pauses and just shakes his head. "Young feller," he said, "some folks just can't tell a joke."

YOU HAVE TO BE CREDIBLE!

Credibility flows from you to the audience. This is part of your verbal and non-verbal message.

This is the scene. A moment before you step up on the podium. Seconds before you begin to speak, what is going through your mind? Are you ready? Financial security could be at stake. Your life could change as a result of this *one* presentation!

You know your subject inside and out. Before you are a couple dozen intelligent corporate executives with impressive credentials, who may be well informed on your subject. *How can you win them over and convey that you know what you are talking about?*

Audiences respond more to a speaker's presence than to a resume' of credentials. So many experts fail when speaking in public because they rub the audience the wrong way. (Not many people like a know-it-all attitude.)

Build a rapport with the audience and lay a foundation of trust. When possible, before the presentation, walk around the room and introduce yourself to as many people as possible. Write their names down and try to remember their faces. Occasionally, during your presentation, refer to them by name. It will make them feel important and make your presentation more personal.

> "To win, we must be believed. To be believed, we must be believable. To be believable, we must tell the truth."
>
> – Gerry Spence, Attorney

There are several ways to establish credibility. Foremost, your level of preparedness will determine your credibility. Enthusiasm, appearance, personal experiences, verbal and body language will reinforce you as a well-chosen presenter. They will feel fortunate to have the access to your knowledge!

Your first 180 seconds of grabbing their attention and making it extremely relevant to your subject is a great start. The more personal the opening, the more credibility you earn! Be natural, be honest, be sincere, be enthusiastic and spontaneous. Your academic credentials simply are not that important.

During your introduction, spare the details. President of, founder of, member of or just your title is plenty. You don't want to overwhelm your audience. Just give them enough information to trust you as a suitable presenter. Your presentation will speak for itself.

THE BODY OF YOUR PRESENTATION

The body of your presentation is the "meat" of what you have to say. Keep this in mind knowing if you are going to lose their attention, this is where it's going to be. However, stay focused on your objectives and the "what's in it for them." Remember, people think four times faster than they speak (except us Southerners, we ...speak....kind...of ...slow), so they will naturally be ahead of you in your presentation. Don't give them time to drift. Include a jolt of business entertainment at nearly every opportunity.

Here are a few interesting statistics on adult retention. The average adult retains:

- 10% of what he reads (read my book)
- 20% of what he hears (listin to my book)

- 30% of what he sees (see my presentation)
- 50% of what he sees and hears (see and hear my presentation)
- 70% of what he says (read the book out loud!)
- 90% of what he says *and* does (come to my training school)
- If this doesn't work, just send me all of your money because there's no hope for you anyway!

If you want to move your audience to action or inspire the group, then get them involved! Get them listening, reading from charts, answering questions out loud, doing projects themselves – that's the path to a successful presentation! Keeping attention during the body of your talk is easier if you use some of the tools of the trade.

Today, more than ever, there are vast selections of tools. Flip charts and markers, overheads, computer equipment, slide projectors, TVs and VCRs and PowerPoint all add punch to presentations. Know how to use your tools. Rehearse your complete presentation with all the tools you intend to use. Variety usually provides for an interesting, quick-moving presentation. The audience will probably be more alert, paying closer attention not to miss anything.

Meanwhile, you move from a picture to a flip chart to a prop relevant to your subject, back to the flip chart (which, by the way, has cheat notes written in pencil that only you can see!). Use what feels right for you to be yourself. The tools are meant to make your job easier and increase the retention and enjoyment of your participants.

Build yourself a "tool box" and get familiar with all your tools. Once you breeze through your talk a few times, you will see just how effective the right tools can be.

TRANSITIONING INTO THE CLOSE

Before moving into your closing, summarize all the principle points and tie the presentation together. Show how you have met each of your objectives one by one. (Continue to reiterate what's in it for them.)

When transitioning into your close, keep in mind the *closing* is the *most significant* part of your talk. A good closing will make participants feel good about what they have just learned. It will inspire them to act. Focus on this statement: *it should inspire them to act.*

The closing should also leave them with something by which to remember you and your key message. Use emotion in your closing as well as a call to action and try to invoke a future challenge. People are yearning to be challenged. Make that challenge.

Most of us are about to explode with ideas that could possibly change our lives and benefit many others. Sometimes all we need is an encouraging word or just to know someone believes in us.

Chuck Norris actually took an "F" in a high school class because he was too embarrassed to give an oral report in front of the class. Later in his youth, one adult encouraged Chuck. He told him of the potential he saw yearning to be expressed. Now he's a TV and movie star and a man who contributes an enormous amount of time to the betterment of our youth. What a tremendous gift the youth of America have gained from Norris as a result of an unknown man that gave Norris the "I-can-do-it" attitude!

Give someone an encouraging word. You never know – *you* could be the little push that someone needs to really achieve greatness. Change the world and change lives!

THE CLOSING SHOULD END WITH A BANG!

The closing is the last and, more importantly, the most powerful opportunity to inspire your participants. Keep it short and keep it positive. Never discuss negatives at this time. Be motivational, assure your participants that their actions do matter and tie these actions to your points and their ultimate success.

Be energetic! Your energy and enthusiasm will inspire the audience more than anything you have to say. If the last thing they see is your enthusiasm, they will leave feeling enthusiastic and ready to act.

SOME FINAL TIPS

NINETY-FIVE PERCENT of how well your presentation is going to go is determined before you even step in front of the audience.

Here's my cheat sheet for planning your first presentation:

1. Define Your Objectives. What is the presentation's purpose? When it's over, what exactly do you want the audience to do?

2. Create Your Closing. Since this is the most important part of your presentation, play your best cards here. This should be the grand finale of all tasks.

3. Create Your Opening. The first 180 seconds is the first impression of you. It's the time to seize your audience's attention and keep it. This is the second most important part of your presentation.

4. Outline Your Presentation Support your case with facts, reasons, proof, examples, testimonies and references.

5. Add Business Entertainment. Remember the secret to maintaining attention is *entertainment*. Add stories, one liners and personal experiences to your presentations where they are relevant. *Do not underestimate this power!*

6. Design Your Visual Aids. Stick men to computerized graphics. Flip charts are really good for nearly any presentation. You are 43 percent more likely to persuade an audience with visuals than without them.

7. Know Your Audience. Make sure they can recognize that this presentation was tailored just for them.

8. Rehearse, Rehearse, Rehearse – then rehearse some more.

I don't mean to drive this into the ground. However; some of these presentations can make you HUNDREDS OF THOUSANDS OF DOLLARS over a lifetime!

It only makes sense to be prepared in the highest regard. In the beginning, the urgency does not set in. However, the week before your presentation is *not* the time to begin preparation.

> # "Never let fear of striking out get in your way."
> — Babe Ruth (1895-1948)
> Professional Baseball Player

A presentation's success depends ultimately upon previous preparation. Without this preparation and rehearsal, the project is destined to fail. *Don't put off preparation.* Remember, it was not raining when Noah built the ark.

If the thought of speaking in public still horrifies you, don't feel alone. However, within you at this moment is the power to do and achieve things you never dreamed possible! You know what you are today, but not what you may be tomorrow! I encourage you to challenge yourself, face your fears and catch the lions! Give up your right to fail! Focus on greatness both in your personal and business life. It's just a matter of choice to succeed!

Perseverance has a magical effect that makes difficulties disappear and obstacles vanish! Always believe in yourself, even when others do not. The fact is you were designed for success. You have power that is unique only in you. No one else in the world may be able to achieve the miraculous feats that only you can bring to reality.

I encourage you to raise your standards over and above what you feel is your comfort zone. Greatness, success, prosperity and happiness are already yours! You hold the power to harness and claim YOUR victory. Nothing can dim you light, which shines from within!

Winners:

Always Have an Idea

Always Say, "I'll Do It!"

See an Answer for Every Problem

Always Say, "I Can"

Look for a Way to Do It

Losers:

Always Have an Excuse

Always Say, "It's Not My Job!"

See a Problem for Every Answer

Always Say, "I Can't"

Look for a Way to Get Out of It

Chapter *16*

Websites & Social Networking

BY ALLISON HESTER

In the mid-1990s, I wrote an article for *Cleaner Times* Magazine explaining what the Internet is. Can you imagine? But at that time, it was new and mysterious. Funniest thing was that I received a number of comments about the article and how it helped them understand this novel mystical universe known as the world wide web.

Today, anybody who's anybody has a website. It's just part of being in business. And as a pressure washing company, you need one too – even if it's just a one-pager. At least it shows potential clients you are serious about your work.

But if your Internet exposure stops with a one-page site, you are missing out on a massive marketing opportunity. Best of all, this opportunity is absolutely free, minus your time. It is the opportunity for social networking.

Social networking is the practice of expanding your business or social contacts by connecting with individuals. While social networking has gone on almost as long as societies themselves have existed, the unparalleled potential of the Internet to promote such connections is only now being fully recognized and exploited, through web-based groups established for that purpose.

BUILDING TRAFFIC

B efore we talk about various forms of social networking, let's talk about search engine optimization (SEO). When someone Googles "pressure washing" (or "power washing" or "pressure cleaning") and the name of your city, you want to be the top listing. Getting there is both an art and a science – and we'll talk about this momentarily – but just know that social networking can play a large role in SEO success.

OK, before we move forward on social networking, let's backtrack and talk about websites.

There are hundreds of books available on designing successful websites. If you want specifics, visit your bookstore or library and you'll find more than you can imagine on the topic. For that reason, I'm not going to go into details on building a website. However, I am going to touch on a few basics that are important to know before talking about social networking.

When creating a website – whether you're creating it yourself or having someone else do it – plan as much of it out ahead of time before putting it together. It's just easier.

Remember that simpler is often better. There are all kinds of cool effects available on websites, but these also take longer to download and may actually drive traffic away.

Just as Steve pointed out before, keep your target market

in mind when creating the design and choosing your words. If you serve residential clients, your look and feel will be different than if you're serving industrial clients.

Look at other people's sites, especially your competitors'. Also, Google terms like "pressure washing" and your city name, and see what comes up and in what order. Then look at the wording in those sites.

Include lots of photos. In the cleaning business, a photo really is worth a thousand words. You can talk about a cleaning process for hours, but it only takes an instant for a good before and after photo to convince a client. However, search engines do no search photos, so be sure to include a caption or other text for the sake of SEO. (You can also include Alt tags, which are hidden terms used to describe what is in the photo.)

Quick sidenote: don't make the photo file size too large. All Internet screens are 72 dpi – i.e., dots per inch – so don't use a 300 dpi file. It will just take longer to download and not look the slightest bit better.

OK, on to SEO. If you build a gorgeous website but do nothing to promote it, you're going to be relying on word of mouth for your marketing. You do need to promote your website by including it on everything you produce, including business cards, flyers, yard signs, direct mail, advertisements and the like. And you probably will generate some traffic through word of mouth.

However, to get the most bang for your buck, you should carefully employ what is known as "organic search engine optimization (SEO)." And actually, I chose my words poorly because the purpose of organic SEO is to get the most bang without spending any extra bucks! Pretty cool, huh?

Organic SEO is defined as the process of making your website get a higher ranking on Google and other search engines through "natural" processes. This is done through the use of keywords, meta tags, website code, and so on. In essense, these are the words – some hidden and some in your headlines and web text – that you or your web designer deliberately include for the search engine robots to pick up on when someone types in a topic on Google, etc.

To learn more, I would suggest going to your local bookstore, grabbing a cup of joe and reading. There is simply too much information to put into a section of a chapter.

What I will share are a couple of other items that can help generate SEO. First, search engines look for other sites that link to your site. That's one reason (among many) that sites like Facebook, Twitter, LinkedIn and MySpace, as well as posting on the industry bulletin boards, are good ideas. (More on these in a bit.) Also, sign up for any business listings you can find, and ask your buddies and family to link their sites to yours.

Finally, search engines honor sites that are constantly updating their content. So change your content. Make sure you plan for this when you create the site. A blog (again, covered momentarily) is an easy way to do this, and the blog itself also adds SEO.

There are also companies that can help you get higher rankings, for a fee. Time is money, so honestly, if you don't have time to do these things yourself, it might be worth looking into hiring someone to do it for you.

And now on to social networking.

LET'S BE FRIENDS

At the spry age of 88-and-a-half, Betty White – famous for her roles in TV shows such as *The Golden Girls* and *Mary Tyler Moore* – made her first appearance on Saturday Night Live in May 2010. In her monologue, she thanked her Facebook fans, confessing that just recently before her appearance she had no idea what Facebook was. Then after she learned what it was, she thought it seemed like something for people with too much time on their hands.

On Facebook, someone started a page called "Betty White on SNL" and began getting fans. Truth be told, I became a "fan." I thought it was funny. (I'm also a fan of things like "not being eaten by bears" and "flipping the pillow to the cool side.") Yes, it's silly. But know what? It landed Betty White a hosting role on SNL. And it got her a Snickers commercial, a new sitcom, movie roles and an amazing comeback at 88 years old!

Now, as a pressure washing business owner, don't expect to land a role on SNL by creating a Facebook page. It is not unreasonable, however, to gain new exposure and business. Underpressure Powerwashers in

My Facebook photo at the time of printing. (It's ok to be personal and even silly.)

California landed the cover of *Cleaner Times* magazine. Know what started it? The company's owner and I became Facebook "friends." I saw some cool photos of a water park volcano that his company cleaned and bada bing. It became an article. The photos were great. It got him the cover.

(I do need to point out that this company has a strong reputation for quality and environmental compliance and has been in the industry for several years. Otherwise, they would not have made the cover!)

I've also talked with companies that have doubled, tripled, even quadrupled their business through Facebook. And frankly, I've gained some writing and graphic design business as well.

How Facebook Can Work for You

In a perfect world, people/companies you'd like to have be your clients would become your Facebook "friends" or "fans," then they'd hire you to do their pressure cleaning work and bam, Facebook success.

In reality, in the nature of this business, it doesn't necessarily work that way. The exception is if you are targeting people in the pressure cleaning business. For instance, if I was selling pressure cleaning widgets for pressure washing contractors, I would want to befriend as many pressure cleaning contractors as possible in hopes of selling them.

However, most contractors are selling cleaning services,

not products, and so getting those potential clients via Facebook is more complicated. However, it's not impossible.

First, focus on befriending others in your industry. I've seen many occasions where pressure-cleaning companies learn of a job in a "friend's" locale and then pass the info along. Some large corporate clients have multiple locations, and again the referral thing comes in handy.

Secondly, if there's a client you want to obtain, see if they are on Facebook and if so, become a friend or a fan. Then POST

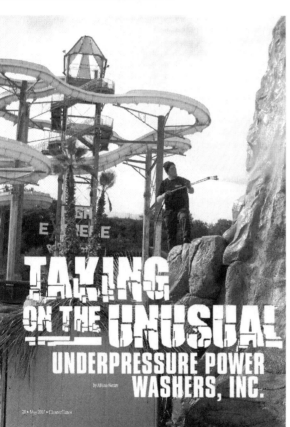

Underpressure Power Washers made the cover of *Cleaner Times* Magazine after the company owner and I became Facebook "friends." I saw these photos on his profile and thought it might make a good article.

stuff on their walls – and not just sales pitches. Respond to their postings. Be more than a friend/fan in name alone. Become an actual friend or fan by letting them know who you are.

As far as your own company's postings, I suggest getting a little personal. I've seen some companies simply post specials on new products. This is ok. However, I suggest doing more than this. Most of the people who are active on Facebook are people who want to connect with other people. Facebook refers to people as "friends" for a reason, and real friends do more than simply present sales pitches.

I am guilty of posting mostly about my family. However, this is my personal Facebook account, not a business account. I've connected with a number of people in the pressure washing industry because I write for this industry, but I'm not using Facebook as a marketing tool. (It has inadvertently turned into one at times, however, because I *have* gained business from it.)

I don't suggest getting too personal or opinionated. For instance, one thing I commonly see that is a big marketing no-no in my opinion is posting comments on politics. This is an area where people get passionate. I get that. However, I would suggest being cautious and respectful if you are going to post a political opinion. I see a lot of governmental official bashing on Facebook, and I cringe when it's on a business site.

Case in point. I recently worked at a charity fundraising event. One of the people attending our event pulled up with a political bumper sticker on his truck – actually it was an anti-administration sticker. A friend who was helping me saw it, and immediately struck up a conversation with the truck's owner. A LOUD conversation. A loud conversation bashing the President, and in front of others. Oh, how I internally groaned. "Please don't make us lose support that could help our charity because you can't keep your political opinion quiet."

On Facebook, I would suggest keeping that in mind. Are you willing to lose a sale because you can't keep quiet about a political happening? Sometimes we are, and I think it's good to stand by our convictions. But if you're just temporarily ticked off about something, think if it's worth losing a client over. (You can always set up a separate personal Facebook account where it theoretically doesn't matter if you offend, although keep in mind your work reputation and character are with you 24/7.)

Also, watch your language. Don't cuss on your postings. That should be common sense, but you might be surprised. Actually, let me just say this – don't cuss when you're working either. I recently took my kids to get a snowcone and there was a "professional" pressure cleaning company washing the house two doors down. While the pressure washer was running, they were cussing left and right. They were probably having a hard time hearing each other with the loud pressure washer next to them. However, their voices clearly carried over to our snow cone experience two lots away. They may have been the most talented pressure cleaning company in Little Rock, but their language read an extreme lack of professionalism, and I posted on Facebook about it!

OK, back to Facebook. I do think it's good to make some

personal posts. Again, make it more than a sales pitch. An occasional posting about looking forward to the weekend, or enjoying your family, or grilling steaks, or whatever lets people connect with you is great. If you're a funny person, use humor.

You can also post personal postings about work. For instance, I've seen stuff like "getting ready to head out for a big new job. God is good!" That simple posting tells me a lot. It tells me the contractor has big clients. It tells me that he has new clients, and therefore is growing. And it tells me that the contractor has at least some sort of faith in God, which, even if I am an atheist (which I am not), this contractor probably strives to work with integrity.

As stressed in other parts of this book, photos are great on Facebook. Again, that's in large part how Underpressure landed the cover of *Cleaner Times*, and that is marketing that money cannot buy. Your clients may refer their friends to you, and they can see your portfolio on Facebook. (Remember, put it on your website too!)

Finally, Facebook helps with your search engine optimization for your website. So even it it's not your thing, just do it!

OTHER SIMILAR SITES

Just a quick note. There are other sites similar to Facebook, such as Twitter (twitter.com) and MySpace (myspace. com). On Twitter, the postings or "Tweets" are shorter than on Facebook, and often considered "micro blogs." (Hang on. Blogging is the next section.) MySpace is very similar to Facebook, but it offers an added blogging feature.

These sites, while they do hold their own, are not as popular as Facebook. But if you've got the time, I would suggest getting on those as well. The cool thing is that you can make your postings to some of these sites automatically show up on the others. In other words, you can connect your Twitter and Facebook together so they automatically update, lessening your effort.

Finally, Linkedin (linkedin.com) is a business oriented social networking site, primarily created for professional networking, that allows business people to include their professional information for their "connections."

Blogging

A final way to market your company and gain business is through the blog. A blog is simply a web site that you create and maintain where you talk about stuff that you are passionate about, or at least that you know something about.

Again, this is a great way to gain search engine points because Google, Yahoo, Bing and other search engines index every word you write. When people look for information on topics, your blog is among those findings.

Although it can be a bit intimidating at first, blogging is pretty simple, especially if you use a pre-made blog site such as blogspot.com or wordpress.com. Best of all, there's no wrong way to do it. (And Steve and I can actually help you write/edit blogs as part of our consulting services.)

While there are no wrong ways to blog, there are some ways that are better than others.

Let me backtrack.

I recently started a personal blog called "Twilights by Allison." I created it on Blogspot and it took me about 30 minutes to set it up. Twilights was created, along with my Twilights facebook page (which now has over 1000 fans), to sell my handmade candles, along

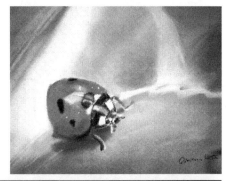

Top: Steve standing in his art gallery.

Middle & Bottom: A couple of my drawings.

with artwork by Steve and me. (Did you know Steve is a FANTASTIC painter?) Ultimately, it's part of my desire to increase autism awareness and gain support for various autism-related organizations I'm involved with. (My son, Ethan, has autism.)

Because promoting autism awareness is a key part of my Twilights blog, I write about life with Ethan. I write about life, period. I write about parenting and marriage and work and my struggles and joys. It's a nice place for me to voice my thoughts. (And I love to write.) But ultimately, it's about selling candles and artwork. Do I write about selling candles? Heck no – (unless it's a specific candle created for a specific cause.) Instead, I'm giving people a chance to put a face and a voice behind my product and the artists involved. I'm helping people understand my passion about autism, and how they can support the cause by buying my products. I'm making the products "human."

If you start a blog for your business, what is your ultimate goal? Making money. Do people want to read about your desire to make money? Of course not. So when writing a blog, follow the guidance that Steve provided in this book. Identify your target and focus on their needs and interests.

In researching the pressure washing blogs that are already out there, I found a few. Most look like they are kind of a side thought…with an occasional post. This is not a bad thing, but for a blog to really pay off and build traffic, posting frequently – at least once or twice a week – is ideal. In fact, the algorithms that search engines use "reward" blogs that update frequently by giving them higher rankings. Like in your website, make sure you use some keywords and choose a blog name that will generate SEO as well. (In other words, don't choose something obscure.)

The blogs for companies selling products, like equipment, detergents, parts, and so on, frankly have it a little easier than those selling pressure washing services. These companies can write all kinds of tips and tricks and specifics on their products. But companies selling cleaning services have more of a challenge.

Again, looking to see what was out there, I found some blogs that primarily had before and after photos. Nothing wrong with those. As Steve and I have both said, photos are imperative in your web presence in this field. So, I think that's a good place to start. But it is just a start.

Again, a blog is a great place for customers to put a face to the name. To get to know you and your company. To make them want to know you and your company. So let's think. As a pressure washing contractor, what could your blog include?

If you're targeting homeowners, you could provide tips on caring for your home. You could write about how you helped someone sell their home. You could write about a party you had on your beautifully-restored deck. You could write about the importance of protecting plants. You could write about your own first home buying experience. You could write about the nice McDonald's employee who provided superior service, and how important customer service is to you. Heck, you could write about your kids or grandkids (just don't overdo it!). You want to present yourself professionally, but you also want to make yourself human. Especially in this market, where women are usually the ones buying your services. Put a face to your company.

If you're targeting fleet companies, what could you write about? Probably not the grandkids. You can write on the importance of professional image. You could write about the courteous truck driver, or the not-so-courteous driver. You could write about your favorite truck stops. You can talk about environmental concerns.

Kitchen exhaust cleaning? Write about your favorite restaurants. (Maybe you could write a blog about each of your customers' restaurants, giving them a plug.) Customer service. Tips and tricks. Fire safety. Restaurants that have burned down.

New Construction? Curb appeal. Professionalism. What to look for in a pressure washing contractor. A challenging job you completed. How you made a customer extremely happy.

In all instances, blogs that talk about the need for using an educated pressure washing company are always good. Then, because you are educated, pick topics that prove you are educated.

People read blogs that use an honest voice that is passionate about a subject. If your blogs are interesting and valuable, readership should grow."

Blogging can also highlight interesting aspects about your company that you wouldn't put into a more formal press release.

Another piece of good news. Most blogs are short. They can even be one paragraph. (These can also be Tweets on Twitter as well, so keep that in mind.)

The most important thing is just to do it. If you are concerned with your writing skills, or if you just don't know how to go about it, keep in mind Steve and I can help you.

You might also just start practicing with a personal blog. If you don't promote, people may never read it, so it doesn't matter if it's good or not. Two friends and I are currently working on our own "just for kicks" blog called "Lost Luggage." It's a good writing exercise, and it's fun.

Again, if you don't promote it, people probably won't read it. But they might. If you've seen the movie "Julie and Julia," you'll know that Julie, a real person, ended up getting a movie made about her because she started a blog about cooking. Of course, she wrote daily, which helped with her SEO.

Nonetheless, if you blog, promote it! Put it on your website. (This also keeps your website fresh, which again helps with Search Engine Optimization!)

If you write a new blog, link it to your Facebook page as an update. Twitter. My Space. Again, SEO. Marketing. And it's absolutely free.

GETTING STARTED

O K, if you are motivated to begin on the things mentioned in this chapter but still aren't sure how to start, here's what we'll do. Go to Facebook (www.facebook.com). If you don't already have an account, the first screen you see will prompt you to set up an account. Do it.

If you already have an account but don't really know how to use it, follow step two.

Once your account is started, do a search for Steve Stephens Consulting. When you find us, hit "Add as Friend."

We will add you as a friend. Note: you can also send a friend request to me, "Allison Hill Hester" as well, but let me warn you. I post a lot about my kids. If you send me a friend request, there's an option to send a note as well. Do that and tell me you're in the pressure cleaning business, and I'll add you.

WARNING: There are spammers on Facebook. If you aren't familiar with someone who sends you a friend request, they may just be trying to get your info. There's a section on Facebook that says "Mutual Friends." I get a lot of requests from people I don't know, but through the mutual friends application I can tell if they are part of a community – such as pressure cleaning.

Finally, if you need help getting the social networking thing going, Steve and I can help. Go to our website – ssconsulting.biz then shoot us an email (or phone call).

Steve and I have been writing for the pressure cleaning industry for many, many years. I've also edited numerous works by pressure cleaning professionals, and I do graphic design, so we can help you write or edit blogs and other marketing materials as well for a small fee.

It may seem silly to pay for social networking help since, after all, the benefit of social networking is it's free. However, if you are wasting hours trying to produce something that you end up not being proud of, that's a more costly choice than letting someone help you get started while you spend your time on growing your business. Our goal is to help teach you to fly, then let you soar on your own.

We want you to succeed! That's what this book is about and that is what we are here for. Let us help you!

Chapter 17

The Setback, Part II

December 22, 2008 – As dusk approached, the peaceful twinkling of holiday illumination along Capital Boulevard in Raleigh, North Carolina, was disastrously overpowered by the churning blue and red flashes of emergency vehicles. Christmas carols dissolved into the blistering shrieks of sirens and agonizing screams of a man being pulled from the vicious wreckage.

And a family gathered, not in celebration, but to learn that their beloved son, brother and friend might never walk or use his hands again.

This excerpt is taken from an article Allison wrote for the December 2009 issue of *Cleaner Times* Magazine. The man in question? Yep. Yours truly.

THE ACCIDENT

I was returning to the office, delivering two 55-gallon drums of hydrochloric acid in the back of my Ford F-150. I usually had chemicals delivered to the shop, but we were running low and I needed them for a job the next day. Also, for some "unknown" reason I decided to tighten the lids with a drum key, something I usually overlooked.

Traffic ahead of me was congested, and knowing I had those drums in back, I decided to slow down. A teenager in a tiny little car with fluorescent lighting along the undercarriage flew up behind me, whipped around my truck, then saw the traffic ahead and panicked, slamming on the brakes.

Rather than flatten the kid like a pancake, which would have surely taken his life, I immediately jerked my wheel to the left into the median and braked with all my might. Wham! The lanyards that were holding the drums broke loose. The horrific sounds of crashing windows were followed by glass propelling like bullets into the back of my head. It looked as though a sling shot thrust the two drums of acid through the back of the cab, over the hood of the truck and onto the highway. (Amazingly not a drop of acid spilled.)

Somewhere in the chaos my airbag deployed, causing the most excruciating pain I have ever experienced in my life. First, the bag smashed my brand new glasses deeply into my face. Then the bag seemed to continue to inflate, bending my neck backwards, farther, farther and still farther. My neck resembled a twig about to be splintered off a tree as I heard the small cracks and snaps. I thought I would surely die. Then I could take no more, and I screamed the most agonizing scream of my life.

Next there were thunderous noises of more shattering glass and screeching tires followed by crashing sounds of impact. Yet I could see nothing. I screamed uncontrollably in pain.

God says He will never give us more than we can handle. When I could take no more pain, He knocked me out of consciousness. Thank you God for that. I will always remember that pain and how You made me sleep! Thank you so very much!

I woke to emergency workers attempting to pull me from the wreckage. I could not feel my arms or legs, but I could definitely feel my neck. Every time they touched me anywhere it seemed somehow to bump or nudge my neck. Even the slightest touch anywhere on my neck caused me to scream uncontrollably and feel like I would pass out again.

My thoughts switched back and forth between wondering if anyone was ok, then thinking about work. I had jobs to do. Clients relying on me. I couldn't let them down.

My mind raced: *How am I gonna get those drums of acid to the job tomorrow? I know. I will borrow David's truck. Or I could rent one. Man, I hope the acid drums did not burst. That will scare everybody. I don't smell any acid so it must be ok. Did anyone else get hurt? I need to get up and get this mess together! Why can't I feel my hands?*

Oh crap. Today is the 22nd. I have to have the job in Virginia done and punched out before Christmas Eve night or they're gonna go nuts!

I am ready to get my face out of all this blood. Where did everybody go? I can't move my legs. What's up with that? I can't move my legs… .

We have a huge day tomorrow. Let's get to the hospital cause I gotta go!

Hey, is everybody OK? I gotta major neck pain! I can't move. Why can't I move?

Man I hope they don't keep me long. The general contractor will not be happy if we don't have the office building across from the hospital completed tomorrow! If they keep me too long I can just swing over there as soon as I get out.

Why can't I move? Man my neck is REALLY hurting. Did anyone else get hurt?

I started to have a panic attack, overwhelmed with everything that I had to get done – or else!

Then an indescribable peace came over me and I could feel God speak to me. "Steve, I got this." And at that point, despite the horrific pain, I knew everything was going to be ok.

THE HOSPITAL

Of course, God's definition of "ok" is not necessarily the same as ours. At the hospital, I learned I had broken the C1 through C7 bones in my neck and crushed my spinal cord. Two days later, on Christmas day, I had two MRIs and CT scans. The doctors determined I needed surgery. The physicians then gave me a one-year window for my nerve endings to heal, meaning whatever feeling I had the following December would likely be where I'd remain for life. As it stands now, I am in extreme, constant pain due to the severe nerve damage that incurred.

That was only part of the bad news. The doctors did not know whether I would ever walk again. The initial thought was that I might possibly be in a wheelchair by the end of the year – if I was lucky. I almost laughed when they told me that. I just couldn't see it.

I spent the next month in the cardiac ward of Wake Medical Hospital. Strangely, despite not being able to use my hands or my legs, this was one of the happiest points of my life.

My left leg was the first limb to regain some movement, and I learned to propel myself in a wheelchair (HA!) with just that leg. Wore the soles of my shoe clean out.

With movement came purpose, and I began wandering from room to room, talking to people, cutting up, playing and talking with others – mostly stroke victims – about how we were going to recover. We talked about why things happened. How we could benefit from these events, and how we could persevere even without the use of our limbs. It ministered to me as much as it did to them.

It became both commonplace and comical for the staff to page me over the hospital intercom system to return to my room for my medication. They really had a time keeping up with me when I learned how to use the elevator!

One day I was just darn tired of wetting on myself and having to have a nurse clean me up. After waiting more than 30 minutes for someone to come help me, I decided to take charge. I put the brake on one wheel of my chair by propelling it against my bed. I had gained use of my left hand fingers but not my arm. Well, I was determined I was not gonna wet on myself again. The plastic urinal was on the bed. I took my left foot and pulled the sheet off the bed while the urinal was coming to me! When I got to the side of the bed, I pulled the sheet. It fell and I caught it with my fingers!

"Praise God!" I shouted. "I'm gonna do this thing!"

My roommate stared in awe. He recently had a stroke and could not speak loudly but could cheer me on in his encouraging whispering voice.

"OK. I have the urinal in my hand, but I can't move it," I thought. "But, it *is* in my hand!"

I continued to scheme. If I stood up I could use the bed to move my arm to where it needs to be then use my fingers!

Stand up? Did I say *stand up*? I *did* say stand up.

So with every fiber of strength I could muster I pushed, pushed and pushed and I felt my bottom leaving the seat of the chair! I was not sitting! Thank you Lord! I was a good foot off my chair.

"MR STEPHENS!!! WHAT ARE YOU DOING!??!?!" A nurse busted me!

"I am getting ready to walk outta here and go pee on YOUR bed!"

She scolded me. The head nurse scolded me. The next day the doctor and the PA scolded me. But from that point they never told me I wouldn't walk again. (Plus when I pressed my button for a nurse they came to me much more quickly!)

THE RETURN HOME

I thought recovering from Fran was the worst experience I could ever imagine. I had no idea at the time, but God was preparing me for something even more challenging.

I returned home in February. My home is in a basement below a flower shop that I currently own. At first, my house was flooded by friends and food and help and support. But quickly people get busy and forget and then it becomes hard. I was stuck in a wheelchair, alone most of the time and unable to get around. For example, well meaning

people would bring me cans of food, but I couldn't use my hands to open them.

This was when the fear began kicking in. How was I going to manage? How could I survive? How could I pressure clean? What about my life's work?

If I didn't have such a good base of friends helping me out and a really, really good client who has made sacrifices, I'd have been out of business.

My recovery continued, and I moved from my wheelchair to a walker. From a walker to braces. From braces to walking without assistance. I also didn't let any grass grow under my feet when it came to work. I traveled to jobsites in my wheelchair, which was challenging – and muddy!

My right arm now has a lot of strength, but my hand is clenched in a fist and cannot open without help. I've got good use of my left hand, but my arm doesn't have much strength. I'm only able to lift a maximum of five pounds. I also struggle daily with intense pain caused by the neurological damage that incurred.

However, I am a walking miracle still under construction of God!

Despite the setbacks, I try to remain optimistic, trusting strongly that everything happens for the best and makes us stronger.

A TURNING POINT

Due to the accident, I am at a turning point in my career, which I hope will allow me to return to my first loves – teaching, speaking, consulting and writing.

Over the years, I've consulted with contractors

I have been able to return to some of my favorite pastimes, such as spending time with my horse Sioux.

from around the country on a variety of topics, from business startup, to specific types of cleaning, to unknown stain elimination. We have been labeled the "problem solvers." Many walls and buildings have been saved because I could remedy stains that were caused by mason contractors, improper cleaning attempts, natural iron salt, mineral deposits, and so on. I'm often able to help contractors do the same, and frequently just by phone.

My ultimate passion is helping companies create business plans, financial plans, marketing plans, customer service procedures and checklists, and even policy and procedure manuals. I built houses for over 12 years and would never attempt to even start without a set of blueprints. Yet business owners attempt to build their businesses without the basics like a business plan.

We all know building a business is harder than building a house! So why even spend the first dime without a hard copy plan of what your goals and purposes are? You will never hit a target you don't have. So while I can certainly help companies in technical areas like the chemistry and specialty stain removal, I feel like my greatest attribute is helping pressure cleaning businesses succeed at business.

WHAT IS UNLUCKY?

Looking at Fran and, more recently, the accident, some people would consider me to be terribly unlucky. However, I am reminded of a story about an incredibly wise man.

The man lived on a farm, was meager, but a very hard worker. He worked the farm with his only son and the one horse they owned. One day, the horse ran away and all the town's people came by to comfort them. They told him how horrible it was that his only horse ran away! How terrible it would be now to work the farm without the horse. They all said how sorry they were that his life was going to be so hard from now on without the horse. The wise man smiled, thanked the people for coming but only said "maybe."

Later that day the horse returned. Not only did it return, it had brought three wild horses with it! The town's people came and laughed and cheered. They said how lucky you are that your horse ran away! You only had one horse, now you have four! Your life is richer; you will not have to work as

hard, now you can make more money. You are a lucky man, they cheered. The wise man thanked them for coming and again only said… "maybe."

His only son

Since the accident, I'm focusing on consulting, training, speaking and writing.

was attempting to train the horses when one threw him and broke both of his legs. Again, the town's people came out to mourn the misfortune of his son. They all spoke of how awful it was that his son was hurt by the horses and how unlucky he was to have had gotten the horses. The man again only said… "maybe."

Later that month, a war broke out and all the young men of the town had to travel off to war, from which most would not return. When the soldiers came to get the son, it was obvious that his legs were broken and he was unable to fight.

The town's people came to the man and told him how lucky he was for his son to be unable to go to war. Again the man replied … "maybe."

The story continues to unfold in our lives as we face each situation. I sincerely hope this story initiates some thought as to obstacles you may be encountering now. (Obstacles… maybe, maybe not!) Hopefully, you will encounter them with an attitude of at least "maybe."

Because life is good. It is our decision as to whether we choose to believe a situation is horrible or if there is a gift somewhere among this mud. General Patton said, "It is not how far you fall but how high you bounce when you hit the bottom." Watch out friends 'cause I am going to need a parachute.

WHAT IS THE SOLUTION?

The answer is simple. Notice I did not say it is easy. In fact, it is downright work. However, the answers are all in the previous material you have read. The irony is that if you are a business getting started, I am at the starting line just like you, from the ground floor. The primary advantage I have is I know this system works. I believe it in my heart and I have seen many contractors pass through our course that are now becoming leaders in this industry!

"There is a difference between knowing the path and walking the path."

Years after Fran hit, my accountant wrote me a letter. He said in the last five years, we had increased our revenue 25 percent each year. Now I am no genius, but did that not double our income, plus twenty-five percent? If that's the case, then why was I so broke? If it cost 25 cents to get around the world, I wouldn't have enough money to get out of sight!

The fact is I am paying debt and disgustingly high amounts of interest from the flood and now my wreck. Thousands of dollars worth of taxes, insurance and other day-to-day costs of running a business.

You bet I have been hit hard! You bet I have hurt. You bet I have and am sacrificing, but let me assure you of this: it is magic that has kept me in business. It is magic that has given my clients the compassion to help me up when they see me fall – literally. It is the magic that allows me to make mistakes and be forgiven. It is the magic that is contagious and is bursting to come out of your heart!

I hope you can feel it because you have it, I promise! God doesn't make average people; people allow themselves to be average. The magic is inside of you. Life is the prize and you are the winner!

Didn't you know that you already won? Don't you know

there was a day you got up, a shot was fired and you took off swimming! Along with several other THOUSANDS of sperm just like you! You are the champion. Only one made it – you!

Can you even fathom the odds that were against you in that race? Have you any idea of the journey you encountered and triumphed? You have already won! Life is your prize! You are special! You are an absolute miracle. There is not another one like you, nor will there ever be.

You have already achieved success just by existing. Just think of what you can achieve now!

This is the place where I should say something like "may the magic be with you." But it already is.

God doesn't make junk. You are capable of great and mighty things, and my staff and I consider it an honor to help pull out your potential. My utmost hope and desire is for you to focus that magic you have on the inside and to take immediate action on the outside.

The magic is much like your success. Unleashed, it is inevitable! You are so unique. Please do not underestimate your power!

I believe in you! We believe in you! You take the action and you will achieve greatness. Live with the magic!

Allow us to help change yor life. I look forward to hearing your story, celebrating your success and seeing you achieve your dreams. Please share your stories with us. You are why we are here.

May God bless your business and give you wisdom as we succeed together.

Remember, success is a choice. *Choose to succeed!*

Contract Cleaner Resource Guide

A.O. Smith Electrical Products Co.
Electric Motors/Blowers
531 N. Fourth St.
Tipp City, OH 45371
937-667-2431
937-667-5030
www.aosmithmotors.com
info@aosmith.com

A.R. North America
Pressure Washer Pumps
140 81st Ave. NE
Fridley, MN 55432
763-398-2008
Fax: 763-398-2009
www.arnorthamerica.com
info@arnorthamerica.com

AaLadin Cleaning Systems
Pressure Cleaning Systems
32584 477th Avenue
Elk Point, SD 57025
605-356-3325; 800-356-3325
Fax: 605-356-2330
www.aaladin.com
info@aaladin.com

Advantage Publishing Co., Inc.
Cleaner Times Magazine
1000 Nix Road
Little Rock , AR 72211
800-525-7233
Fax: 501-280-9233
www.cleanertimes.com

Alkota Cleaning Systems
Pressure Washing Equipment Mfr.
105 Broad Street
Alcester, SD 57001
605-934-2222; 800-255-6823
Fax: 605-934-1746
www.alkota.com
info@alkota.com

American Made Cleaners
High Pressure Washers
610 E. Cedar St.
Beresford, SD 57004
(605) 763-5100
Fax (605) 763- 5201
www.amclean.com
amclean@bmtc.net

American Building Rest. Prod., Inc.
Restoration & Preservation Chemicals
9720 S. 60th St.
Franklin, WI 53132
414-421-4125; 800-346-7532
Fax: 414-421-8696
www.abrp.com
abrp@abrp.com

American Honda Motor Co., Inc.
Pressure Washer Engines
4900 Marconi Dr.
Alpharetta, GA 30005
770-497-6400
Fax: 678-339-2670
www.honda.com

American Water Broom
Water Brooms
3565 McCall Pl.
Atlanta, GA 30340
770-451-2000; 800-241-6565
Fax: 770-455-4478
info@waterbrooms.com

Anderson Metals Corp, Inc.
*Manufacturer of Brass Fittings, Valves
and Pipe Nipples*
1701 Southern Road
Tel: 816-471-2600
Fax: 816-472-8700
www.andersonmetals.com
info@andersonmetals.com

Aqua Blast Corp.
High Pressure Cleaning Units
1025 W Commerce
PO Box 547
Decatur, IN 46733
800-338-7373
Fax: 260-728-4517
www.aquablast.com

Arthur Products Co.
Water Blasting Nozzles
1140 Industrial Parkway
Medina, Ohio 44256
330.725.4905; 800-322-0510
Fax: 330.722.2698
www.arthurproducts.com
apc@apclsq.com

Awning Rejuvenation Systems Intl.
Awning Cleaners & Sealers
6732 N.W. 20th Ave.
Fort Lauderdale, FL 33309
800-776-5664
Fax: 954-971-0193
www.awningcleaning.com
arsi@bellsouth.net

Barens, Inc.
Pressure Washer Parts & Accessories
PO Box 269
Seneca, PA 16346
800-676-0607
Fax: 800-326-7146
www.barens.com
dave@barens.com

BE Pressure Supply, Inc.
Full Line of Industrial Power Equipment
1264 Riverside Rd.
Abbotsford, BC, Canada V2S 7P3
604-850-6662
Fax: 604-850-8886
www.begroup.cc
braber@uniserv.com

Brewer Products Co.
Pavement Products and Equipment
PO Box 62065
Cincinnati, OH 45262
513-577-7200
Fax: 513-577-7210
www.BrewerProducts.com
info@brewerproducts.com

Comet USA
Industrial Pump Products
12571 Oliver Avenue, Ste 300
Burnsville, MN 55337
952-707-1894
800-708-1894
Fax: 888-708-1895
www.cometpump.com
cometpump@cometpump.com

Consolidated Chemex Corp.
Vehicle Cleaning Systems & Products
235 Jersey Avenue
New Brunswick, NJ 08901
800-257-7876
732-828-7676
Fax: 732-828-8677
www.chemexcorp.net

Contam-Away Blasting Systems
Soda Blasting Systems
5000 Brittonfield Pkwy.
East Syracuse, NY 13057
315-437-6400 ext. 2830
Fax: 315-437-9800
http://www.obg.com/solutions/tech/contamaway.aspx
info@obg.com

Control Switches Intl. Inc.
Control Switches
2425 Miramar Ave.
Long Beach, CA 90815
562-498-7331; 800-521-1677
Fax: 562-498-5894
www.controlswitches.com

Coxreels Inc.
Industrial Grade Hose Reels
6720 S Clementine Ct.
Tempe, AZ 85283
480-820-6396; 800-269-7335
Fax: 800-229-7335
www.coxreels.com
info@coxreels.com

Cuda Cleaning Systems
Aqueous Parts Washers
51804 Industrial Dr.
Calumet, MI 49913
888-319-0882
Fax: 888-805-9657
www.cudausa.com
info@cudausa.com

Cyclone Blasters
Sandblast & Abrasive Blast Equip.
P.O. Box 815
Dowagiac Michigan 49047
269-782-9670
Fax: 269-782-9623
http://www.cycloneblasters.com

Diedrich Technologies Inc.
New Masonry Cleaning, Restoration
& Water Repellent Products
7373 S. 6th St.
Oak Creek, WI 53154
800-323-3565
Fax: 414-764-6993
www.diedrichtechnologies.com

Dirt Killer Pressure Washers
Pressure Washers, Soaps &
Accessories
1708 Whitehead Road
Baltimore, Maryland 21207
410-944-9966
8oo-544-1188
Fax: 410-944-8866
www.dirtkiller.com
info@dirtkiller.com

Do It Right, Inc.
Awning Cleaners & Sealers
501 N. Newport Ave.
Tampa, FL 33606
800-364-3772
Fax: 813.258.9347
www.doitrightonline.com
paul@awningcleaningpro.com

Draygon Enterprises, Inc.
Floor Cleaning Tools & Wastewater
Disposal Systems
15 Blake Way
Osprey, FL
941-485-9676; 800-724-3610:
Fax 941-485-3456
www.draygon.com
Questions@draygon.com

Duckback Products, Inc.
Wood and Concrete Cleaners, Stains
& Sealers
PO Box 980
Chico, CA 95927
800-825-5382
Fax: 530-343-3283
www.superdeck.com
customerservice@superdeck.com

EDI Distributors, Inc.
Pressure Washing Pump Mfr. &
Equipment Distributor
20 Lakeside Ave.
Cherry Hill, NJ 08003
800-433-2033
Fax: 856-428-2549
http://www.edidistributors.com/
info@edidistributors.com

Environmental Solutions Corp.
Self Contained Cleaning Systems
495 Oak Road
Ocala, FL 34472
800-277-3279; 352-680-0400
Fax: 352-680-9278
www.pressureisland.com

Environmental Process Systems
Water Treatment Equipment
PO Box 342
Willow Spring, NC 27593
Phone: 919-264-3661
Fax: 919-573-9573
www.epsiusa.com/epsi/index.asp
info@epsiusa.com

EnviroSpec
Pressure Washing Equipment &
Supply Catalog
Rt. 1 Box 12D
Homerville, GA 31634
800-346-4876
Fax: 912-487-18889
www.envirospec.com
sales@envirospec.com

EPPS Products
High Pressure Cleaning Equipment
Mfr.
RR #4
Clinton, ON, Canada N0M 1L0
519-233-3418
Fax: 519-233-3474
www.eppsproducts.com
epps@eppsproducts.com

Ericson Manufacturing Company
Electrical Cords & Equipment
4215 Hamann Parkway
Willoughby, OH 44094
800-ERICSON
Fax: 440-951-1867
www.ericson.com
info@ericson.com

Etowah Chemical
Pressure Washer Chemicals
2618 Forrest Avenue
Gadsden, AL 35904
800-848-8541
Fax: 256-547-7555
http://www.etowahchemicals.com

F.C. Kingston Company
Industrial Valves
23201 Normandie Ave.
Torrance, CA 90501
866-628-8287; 310-326-8287
Fax: 866-997-0500
www.fckingston.com
sales@kingstonvalve.com

Farley's, Inc.
Pressure Washer & Coil Mfr.
PO Box 1209
Siloam Springs, AR 72761
479-524-9594; 800-522-2645
Fax: 479-524-4570
www.farleysinc.com/
faleysinc@bstream.com

Florida Pneumatic Mfg.
Air Tool Mfr.
851 Jupiter Park Ln.
Jupiter, FL 33458
561-744-9500; 800-327-9403
Fax: 561-575-5574
www.florida-pneumatic.com

Freemyer Industrial Pressure
Industrial Cleaning Equipment Mfr.
1500 N Main St., Suite 127
Fort Worth, TX 76164
817-548-5010
Fax: 817-284-2783
www.indpress.com

Gardner Denver Water Jetting Systems, Inc.
Water Jetting Equipment
12300 N. Houston-Rosslyn Rd.
Houston, TX 77086
281-448-5800; 800-231-3628
Fax: 281-448-7500
www.waterjetting.com
mktg@waterjetting.com

General Pump
Pressure Washer Pumps
1174 Northland Dr.
Mendota Heights, MN 55120
651-454-6500
Fax: 651-454-8015
www.generalpump.com
info@gpcompanies.com

Giant Industries
Pressure Washer Pumps & Accessories
900 N. Westwood Ave
Toledo, OH 43607
419-531-4600
Fax: 419-531-6836
www.giantpumps.com
sales@giantpumps.com

Global Equipment, Wheelwash Division
Wheel Wash Cleaning Systems
Kiely Distribution Co.
700 McClellan Street
Long Branch, NJ 07740
732-921-7934
Fax: 732-403-8012
www.wheelwash.com
btaylor@wheelwash.us.com

Graffiti Solutions, Inc.
Graffiti Removal Products
2263 McKnight Road North, Suite 2
North Saint Paul, MN 55109
(651) 777-0849; 800-891-0091
Fax: 651-770-9951
www.graffitisolutionsusa.com
gshipshock@graffitisolutions.com

Graymills
Industrial Pumps, Filters & Accessories
3705 N. Lincoln Avenue
Chicago, IL 60613
773-248-6825
Fax: -800-478-8673
www.graymills.com
info@graymills.com

Great Plains
Wholesale Power Equipment
2800 Southcross Dr. West
Burnsville, MN 55306
800-525-9716
Fax: 866-641-2568
www.gpcatalog.com
gpcatalog@northerntool.com

Grinnell Water Systems, Inc.
1692 Riverdale Rd.
Ozark, MO 65721
800-424-4930
Fax: 417-485-8500

Hago Manufacturing Co., Inc.
Precision Nozzles
1120 Glove Ave.
Mountainside, NJ 07092
908-232-8687; 800-710-HAGO
Fax: 908-232-7246
www.hagonozzles.com
hago@danfoss.com

Hannay Reels
Industrial Hose Reels
553 State Route 143
Westerlo, NY 12193
877-GO-REELS
Fax: 800-REELING
www.hannay.com
reels@hannay.com

Harben Inc.
Pressure Washing Equipment, Parts &
Accessories
PO Box 2250
Cumming, GA 30028
800-327-5387; 770-889-9535
Fax: 770-887-9411
www.harben.com
harbeninc@aol.com

Higher Power Supplies
Pressure Washing Equipment & Supply
Catalog
6320 Evergreen Way, Suite 101
Everett, WA 98203
877-389-3131
Fax: 425-353-9058
www.higherpowersupplies.com
sales@higherpowersupplies.com

Hoosier Wheel and Stamping
Pneumatic & Semi-Pneumatic
Wheel Assemblies
P.O.Box 6447
Evansville, IN 47719
812-421-6900; 877-206-4762
Fax: 812-421-6908
www.hoosierwheel.com
sales@hoosierwheel.com

Hotsy
Pressure Washer Systems, Parts &
Accessories Mfr.
21 Inverness Way East
Englewood, CO 80112
800-525-1976; 303-792-5200
Fax: 303-792-0547
www.hotsy.com
info@hotsy.com

HPW Inc.
Turnkey Pressure Washing
Systems
201 Spinnaker Way, Unit 13
Concord, ON, Canada L4K 4C6
905-761-8822
Fax: 905-761-8722
http://www.hpwincorporated.com

HydraMotion Cleaning Systems
Sidewinder Flat Surface Cleaner
Mfr.
401 E. Fourth St.
Bridgeport, PA 19405
800-726-1526
Fax: 610-239-7863
www.hydramotion.us/
hydrasales@aol.com

Hydro Engineering, Inc.
*Pressure Washing and Wastewater
Equipment Systems*
865 W 2600 South
SLC, UT 84119
800-247-8424
Fax: 801-972-3265
www.hydroblaster.com

Hydro Tek Systems, Inc.
*Pressure Washing Equipment &
Accessories*
10418 Enterprise Dr.
Redlands, CA 92374
909-799-9222; 800-274-9376
Fax: 909-799-9888
www.hydroteksystems.com
sales@hydroteksystems.com

Hydro-Quip Mfg. & Supply
Pressure Washer Mfr.
1923 Smith St.
Baton Rouge, LA 70806
225-924-2444
www.hydro-quip.com

Hypro Corporation
Pump Mfr.
375 Fifth Ave. NW
New Brighton, MN 55112
800-424-9776
Fax: 800-323-6496
www.hypropumps.com

Jenny Products, Inc.
Steam Cleaners
850 North Pleasant Avenue
Somerset, PA 15501
814-445-3400
Fax: 814-445-2280
www.steamjenny.com

Jet Edge
*Water Jetting Equipment, Pumps
& Accessories*
10270 43rd St. N.E.
St. Michael, MN 55376-8427
763-497-8700; 800-538-3343
Fax: 763-497-8701
www.jetedge.com
sales@jetedge.com

Jetstream of Houston, LLP
Waterblasting Systems
5905 Thomas Road
Houston, TX 77041
832-590-1300; 800-231-8192
832-590-1304
www.waterblast.com
sales@waterblast.com

JGB Enterprises, Inc.
Hose, Fittings &Valves
115 Metropolitan Drive
Liverpool, New York 13088
(315) 451-2770
Fax (315) 451-8503
www.jgbhose.com
jgb@jgbhose.com

K & E Chemical Co.
Masonry Restoration Products
3960 East 93rd Street
Cleveland, Ohio 44105
Tel: 800.331.1696
Fax: 216.341.1651
http://www.klenztone.com

Karcher
Pressure Washer Manufacturer
4275 NW Pacific Rim Blvd
Camas, WA 98607
Phone: (800) 537-4129
www.karcher-usa.com
info@karcherna.com

KMT Aqua-Dyne Inc.
Water Blasting Equipment & Parts
635 West 12th Street
Baxter Springs, KS 66713
800)-26-9274
Fax:(620) 856-5050
www.aqua-dyne.com
sales@aqua-dyne.com

KO Manufacturing, Inc.
Professional Cleaning Detergents
2720 E. Division Street
Springfield, MO 65803
417-866-8000; 800-777-7627
Fax: 417-866-2662
www.komfg.com

Landa Cleaning Systems
Pressure Washer Mfr.
800-526-3248 ext. 2
www.landa.com
info@landa.com

Largo Cleaning Systems
Pressure Washer Manufacturer
40 Sevier Lane
Decaturville, TN 38329
731-852-2324; 800-626-7384
gcalargo.com
sales@gcalargo.com

Maury Enterprises
Pressure Washer Manufacturer
1625 NW 1st CT.
Boca Raton, FL 33432-1721
561-394-4930; 800-93-PUMPS
Fax: 561-394-0091
www.pressurecleaners.com

Mi-T-M Corp.
Pressure Washer Manufacturer
8650 Enterprise Dr.
Peosta, IA 52068
563-556-7484
www.mitm.com

MSI Mobile Systems, Inc.
Pressure Washer Manufacturer,
Detergents & Parts
615-885-4343; 888-649-6449
www.mobileclean.com
sales@mobileclean.com

Mosmatic Corp.
Flat Surface & Roof Cleaners, Swivels
8313-196th Ave.
P.O.Box 400
Bristol, WI 53104
800-788-9880
Fax: 262-857-2421
www.mosmatic.com
swivels@mosmatic.com

National Pride Equipment
Carwash Equipment & Parts
1266 Middle Rowsburg Road
P.O. Box 467
Ashland, OH 44805
419-289-2886; 800-537-6788
419-281-5526
www.nationalpridecarwash.com
rsummers@nationalpridecarwash.com

New Again Corp.
Professional Cleaning Products
813-247-4969; 866-639-2424
Fax: 813-877-6341
www.newagain.net
info@newagain.net

Nilfisk-ALTO
Pressure Washers & Accessories
14600 21st Avenue North
Plymouth, MN 55447
877-366-2589\
http://www.nilfisk-alto.us/
info@altocsi.com

NLB Corp.
Waterjetting Equipment
29830 Beck Rd.
Wixom, MI 48393
248-624-555
Fax: 248-624-0908
www.nlbcorb.com
nlbmktg@nlbusa.com

Parker Polyflex Operations
Hose, Valves & Other Accessories
6035 Parkland Blvd
Cleveland, OH 44124
216-896-3000; 800-272-7537
Fax: 216-896-4000
www.parker.com

Pressure Power Systems, Inc.
Vacuboom Mfr.
P.O. Box 917
Kernersville, NC 27285 (USA)
336-996-5585
Fax: 336-996-6217
www.vacuboom.com

Pressure Pro
Pressure Washing Equipment Mfr.
7300 Commercial Cir.
Ft. Pierce, FL 34951
772-461-4486
Fax: 888-872-0365
www.pressure-pro.com
sales@pressurepro.com

PSC Cleaning Systems
Pressure Washer Mfr.
3300 Steeles Ave.
West Concord, Ontario, Canada, L4K 2Y4
905-761-1733; 800-246-9689
Fax: 905-738-6168
www.pscclean.com/
info@pscclean.com

Ramteq, Inc.
Pressure Washer Mfr.
14275 Northwest Freeway
Houston, TX 77040
713-983-6400
Fax: 713-893-6405
www.ramteq.com

Red Arrow Manufacturing
Pressure Washers & Fleet Cleaning Equipment
1761 East 64th Avenue
Denver, CO 80229
303-375-0908; 800-783-0908
Fax: 303-375-0909
www.redarrowmfg.com

Reel Quick
Hose Reels
P.O. Box 22640
Lincoln, NE 68542
866-523-2363
www.rapidreel.com

Ronco Plastics Inc.
Water Tanks
15022 Parkway Loop Suite B
Tustin, CA. 92780
714-259-1385
Fax: 714-259-0759
www.ronco-plastics.com
sheilas@ronco-plastics.net

Ron-Vik, Inc.
Filters & Strainers
800 Colorado Avenue South
Minneapolis, MN 55416
763-545-0276; 800-328-0598
Fax: 763.545.0142
www.ron-vik.com
Sales@Ron-Vik.com

Safway
Scaffolding
N19 W24200 Riverwood Drive
Waukesha, WI 53188
262-523-6500; 800-558-4772
www.safway.com

Schieffer Co. Intl. LC
Industrial Hose
8545 Kapp Drive
Dubuque/Peosta, IA 52068
563-583-4758
563-583-7743
jtheis@schefferusa.com

Shamrock Tools
Pipe Cleaning Nozzles, Hoses &
Accessories
10928 S. Choctaw Dr.
Baton Rouge LA 70815
225-275-7696; 800-6337696
Fax: 225-275-1340
http://shamrocktools.com/

Sioux Corporation
Steam Cleaners
One Sioux Plaza
Beresford, SD 57004-1500
605-763-3333
Fax: 605-763-3334
www.sioux.com
email@sioux.com

Spartan Mfg. Corporation (SMC)
Steam Cleaners & Pressure Washing
Equipment
P.O. Box 917
Kernersville, NC 27285-0917
336-996-5585
Fax: 336-996-6217
www.smcwashers.com
SpartanSales@SpartanManuf.com

Spraying Systems Co.
Nozzles
P.O. Box 7900
Wheaton, Illinois 60187-7901
USA
Phone (630) 665-5000
Fax (630) 260-0842
www.spray.com
Email info@spray.com

Spraymart
Supplier of Pressure Washer
Aftermarket & Replacement Parts
603 North Monitor Rd
Springdale, AR 72764
800.752.0177
www.spraymart.com
sales@Spraymart.com

Steel Eagle
Flat Surface Cleaners, Hose
Reels, Detergents & Other
Pressure Washer Accessories
32586 477th Ave.
Elk Point, SD 57025
605-356-2918; 800-447-3924
605-356-2144
www.steeleagel.com

Stoneage Waterjet Tools
Waterjetting Nozzles
466 S Skylane Drive
Durango, CO 81303
970-259-2869; 866-795-1586
Fax: 970-259-2868
www.stoneage.com
customerservice@stoneagetools.
com

Summit Hose Reels
High Pressure Hose Reels
10586 East 59th Street
Indianapolis, IN 46236
317-823-2848; 800-622-7404
Fax: 317-823-2850
www.summithosereels.com
info@summithosereels.com

Sun Brite Supply
Pressure Washer Equipment &
Accessories Catalog Supplier
877-5-SUPPLY
http://sunbrite.stores.yahoo.net/

Suttner America
Pressure Washer Accessories &
Components
14864 West Ridge Lane
Dubuque, IA 52003
563-556-3212; 800-831-0660
Fax: 800.821.0660
www.suttner.com
sales@suttner.com

Technology Research Corporaton
GFCIs
5250 140th Hwy. 20 West
Clearwater, FL 33760
800-780-4324
Fax: 727-530-7375
www.trci.net
productinfo@trci.net

Tilton Equipment Company
Pressure Washer Mfr.
www.tiltonequipment.com

Titan Products, Inc.
Hose Reels
www.titanprod.com
P.O. Box 1538
Largo, Florida 33779
727-531-1770
727-530-1502
E-mail: sales@titanprod.com

Tommy Gate Company
Lift Gates
1210 Lincoln Way
Woodbine, IA 51579
800-LIFTGATE
www.tommygate.com
info@tommygate.com

Tuthill Coupling Group – Hansen
Coupling Fittings & Accessories
http://www.tuthill.com

U.S. Para Plate Corporation
High Performance Valves &
Pressure Regulators
1100 Page Street
Bristol, VA 24201
276-591-4837
Fax: 276-466-4256
usparaplate.com/

Udor USA
Diaphragm & Plunger Pumps
500 Apollo Drive
Lino Lakes, MN 55014
651-785-0666
Fax: 800-732-2670
www.udorusa.com
Info@udorusa.com

Ultrasonics International Corp.
Ultrasonic Cleaning Systems
800.500.2544
http://sonicpro.com
sales@sonicpro.com

U.S. Jetting, Inc.
High Pressure Waterjetting Systems
850 McFarland Road
Alpharetta, GA 30004
Sales: 800-538-8464
Local: 770-740-9917
http:usjetting.com

V-Seal/Tara Distribution Group
Concrete Sealers
9042 Cotter Street
Lewis Center, Ohio 43035
614-754-4777; 877-73V-SEAL
www.vseal.com
info@vseal.com

Vector Laboratories
Detergents & Accessories
316 Alexander Street
Youngstown, Ohio 44502
800-331-0347
www.vectorchemicals.com
vectorchemicals@aol.com

Walters Insurance Agency
Pressure Washing Insurance
1525 Freeport Road
Natrona Heights, PA 15065
724-2242505
724-226-1220
www.walterinsuranceagency.com

Water & Process Technologies
*Water Treatment, Wastewater
Treatment and Process Systems
Solutions*
4545 Patent Road
Norfolk, Virgina 23502
800-446-8004
Fax: 562-948-4640
www.gewater.com

Water Maze
Water Treatment Systems
Tel 800-347-6116
Fax 800-535-9164
Email info@wmaze.com
www.wmaze.com

Water Treatment Techologies
Water Treatment Systems
1071 Evergreen Lane
Vista, CA 92084
760-630-9425; 800-420-6662
Fax: 760-630-0837
www.watertreatmenttech.com
edbonilla@watertreatmenttech.com

Wayne Combustion Systems
Burners
 801 Glasgow Ave.
Fort Wayne, IN 46803
260-425-9200; 800-443-4625
Fax: 260-424-0904
www.waynecombustion.com

Whisper Wash
Rotary Spray Systems
Suite 305
4400 118th Avenue North
Clearwater, FL 33762
727-573-1292; 800-898-6146
Fax: 727-572-1292
www.whisperwash.com
brad@autoxtc.com

Whitco Cleaning Systems
High Pressure Cleaning Equipment
www.whitcoinc.com

Wolman Wood Care Products
Wood Restoration Products
11 E. Hawthorn Pkwy.
Vernon Hills, IL 60061
847-367-7700
Fax: 847-816-2330
www.wolman.com

Wood Iron Wood Finishes, Inc.
Wood Restoration Products
10475 Irma Drive, Unit 7
Northglenn, CO 80233-4227
303-650-1681; 888-WOODIRON
Fax: 303-428-3004
www.woodiron.com
info@woodiron.com

Xterior Sales & Service Inc.
X-Jet Nozzle
142 Annaron Ct
Raleigh, NC 27603
919-779-7905; 800-983-7467
Fax: (919) 779-7784
www.xterior.com

Yanmar Diesel America Corp.
Engine Manufacturer
101 International Parkway
Adairsville, GA 30103
770.877.9894
Fax: 770.877.9009
www.yanmar.com

www.stevestephens.biz